The Fred. Olsen Line
and its Passenger Ships

The Fred. Olsen Line and its Passenger Ships

by
Anthony Cooke

Published by
Carmania Press
PO Box 56435, London, SE3 0SZ.

Artwork production by Alan Kittridge.
Printed by The Amadeus Press, Cleckheaton, West Yorkshire.

ISBN 978-0-9543666-7-4. First published 2007

Contents

FRONT COVER
Stephen J. Card's painting captures the beauty of Fred. Olsen's stylish and innovative *Black Prince (i)* of 1938, whose career was cut sadly short by the Second World War.

BACK COVER (top)
The spacious and comfortable *Black Watch (iii)*, seen off Portoferraio on the island of Elba during a Mediterranean cruise, is often employed on longer voyages, including Round the World cruises. *(Clive Harvey)*

BACK COVER (bottom)
Braemar (ii) regularly spends the winter months cruising in the Caribbean and in South American waters. This photograph was taken while she was on the River Amazon in November, 2002. *(Clive Harvey)*

FRONTISPIECE
For many years, Fred. Olsen ships were given figureheads or other bow decorations specially commissioned from Norwegian artists. That on *Black Prince (ii)* is by Kjell Rasmussen and depicts the ballerina Anne Borg. *(Bruce Peter)*

Introduction

I first sailed on a Fred. Olsen ship in 1993 when I took a Norwegian cruise on *Black Prince (ii)*. Like many of her passengers before and since, I found the atmosphere on board particularly congenial. Since then, I have sailed on her and on the other members of the Fred. Olsen Cruise Lines fleet many times, both as a passenger and as a lecturer, and I have found them all full of character, sometimes quirky but always likeable.

This book is specifically about the many passenger ships which, over the years, have served the various companies controlled by Fred. Olsen & Co. of Oslo. But it should not be forgotten that there has always been much more to the Olsen business than just the passenger vessels, though these have usually been the aspect of the group which has been most familiar to the general public. There have, for instance, been generations of cargo ships; the tankers of the Knock Group, including the huge ships which act as stationary storage vessels in the Gulf (one of them, the 1,504 feet long *Knock Nevis* is the largest ship in the World); the shipbuilding and repairing interests, both in Norway and Great Britain, though these have been greatly reduced as the European shipbuilding industry has declined; the oil rigs; the wind farms; the experiment with tidal power; the Timex watch manufacturing business; the Tusenfryd pleasure park some miles out of Oslo, which attracts half a million visitors a year (this in a country of 4.7 million inhabitants); the investments in airlines, now sold; the logistics business; the land, hotel, restaurant and golf course on La Gomera, one of the Canary Islands – the list is formidable.

Several strands run through the story. It is a Norwegian family saga, though with strong British links, and there is pride in the family's Norwegian seafaring heritage. Shipowning is a risky and competitive trade and the Olsens have always been strong-minded business people. They have also been open to innovation, responsible, for instance, for some important developments in cargo handling, and have owned some of the most ingenious and adaptable multi-purpose ships of recent times. But there is also an aesthetic streak in this story. This can be seen in the beauty of many of the Olsen vessels; the revival of the old custom of adorning ships with figureheads; the involvement of members of the Olsen family in the decoration and furnishing of the present-day cruise ships; and the various commissions which helped to establish the career of a young architect called Norman Foster.

It is the passenger ships which concern us here. There has been a huge variety of them: the tiny steamers which used to criss-cross the North Sea; the later, more luxurious North Sea ships; the Skagerak ferries; the ferries and now the catamarans (and a trimaran) which dash around the Canary Islands in such a spectacular fashion; other ferries linking Morocco with Europe; and, above all, the cruise ships. As I found on that first *Black Prince (ii)* voyage, Fred. Olsen Cruise Lines have a very individual character. They have hitherto concentrated mainly on the British market and their ships, although growing in size over the years, are still much smaller than the behemoths which many other companies have introduced in recent times. Most Olsen passengers like it that way and it is undoubtedly one of the several reasons why there is often such a friendly atmosphere on board. The *Balmoral*, the latest addition to the fleet, is the largest Olsen cruise ship yet but she is still of a manageable size and she too promises to offer her passengers the kind of sociable, congenial cruises for which the line has become so well-known.

Anthony Cooke,
Greenwich,
London.
October, 2007.

The headquarters of Fred. Olsen & Co. are housed at 2, Fred. Olsens Gate, Oslo. Part of the building dates back to the early eighteenth century and has very elegant, very Norwegian interiors. *(Fred. Olsen & Co.)*

Acknowledgements

I am extremely grateful to Mr. Fred. Olsen for giving his blessing to my suggestion that I write a history of his family's passenger ships and their services. The more I research the subject, the more remarkable I think that story is. In addition, I have had a great deal of help from other people in the Fred. Olsen organisation. I am particularly grateful to Nigel Lingard, who is the Marketing Director of Fred. Olsen Cruise Lines, and to Wendy Hooper-Greenhill, who is their Publicity Manager. Both are based in Ipswich. Also very helpful have been Aase Kornstad, Fridthjov Haarvardsson, Rolf Holme and Knut Klippenberg at the group's head office in Oslo; Arne Valberg at Hvitsten; and also Harald Bråthen. The co-operation of all these people has made this book possible.

Many others have helped, particularly by lending photographs and other material. I must especially mention the late Laurence Dunn and his wife Jennifer, dear friends and wonderful sources of information, encouragement and hospitality. In that connection, I must also include Peter Newall who now owns Laurence's photograph collection and has so generously made material available from his own archives. John Sutherland, who has a unique knowledge of the figureheads which distinguished Olsen ships for many years, has also been extraordinarily helpful, as have Bruce Peter, one of the great authorities on Scandinavian passenger vessels, and Ambrose Greenway, whose book on North Sea passenger ships is a classic and who represents the shipping industry so assiduously in Parliament. Maurizio Eliseo, although a very busy shipping professional and historian, has given an enormous amount of time and effort to the production of this book. And the fine marine artist Stephen Card has made a beautiful painting of a beautiful ship for its cover. To all of these good friends, I give my grateful thanks.

In addition, other friends in various countries have helped this project in different ways, often very generously. They include Ahmet Anadolu; Dag Bakka, Jr.; Declan Barriskill of Guildhall Library in the City of London; Stefan and Petra Behn; Jonathan Boonzaier; Ian Boyle; Luís Miguel Correia; Timothy J. Dacey; Tony Davis; Martin Grant; Clive Harvey; Frank Heine: Peter Knego; Captain Roland Parent; Paolo Piccione; Ted Scull; Der Scutt; and Jörgen Waerhaug.

A few of the illustrations in this book have been taken from postcards issued, often many years ago, by Fred. Olsen & Co. or associated companies. Where these have been made available for reproduction by private collectors, I have attributed them accordingly.

Primary Sources:
Lloyd's Confidential Index.
Lloyd's Register.
Lloyd's Shipping Index.
Lloyd's Voyage Records.
Lloyd's Weekly Casualty Reports.
Various brochures and timetables.

Periodicals:
Cruise Business Review.
Ferries: Das Fährschiffahrtsmagazin.
Linjen (the house journal of Fred. Olsen & Co.).
Lloyd's List.
Marine News (the journal of The World Ship Society).
Sea Breezes.
Sea Lines (the journal of the Ocean Liner Society).
Shipping Today & Yesterday.
Ships in Focus Record.
Ships Monthly.
Skipet (the journal of Norsk Skipsfartshistorisk Selskap).
Steamboat Bill (the journal of The Steamship Historical Society of America).
The Motor Ship.
The Times.

Books:
Bergenske: Byen og Selskapet (Dag Bakka, Jr., Seagull Publishing, Bergen, 1993).
A Century of North Sea Passenger Steamers (Ambrose Greenway, Ian Allan, Shepperton, 1986).
Ferries 2004, Southern Europe (John May and William Mayes, Overview Press, Windsor, 2004).
Ferry Tales, Tyne – Norway Voyages, 1864-2001 (Dick Keys and Ken Smith, Tyne Bridge Publishing, Newcastle upon Tyne, 2002).
Fred. Olsen / Bergen Line (N. L. Middlemiss, Shield Publications, Ltd., Newcastle upon Tyne, 1990).
Fred. Olsen Lines, Historiske oversikter og Liste over skip og Offshore Fartøyer, 1848-1994 (Fred. Olsen & Co., Oslo, 1994).
Liners & Cruise Ships, vols. 1, 2 and 3 (Anthony Cooke, Carmania Press, London, 1996 -2003).
Mediterranean Shipping (Laurence Dunn, Carmania Press, London, 1999).
Norman Foster, Works 1 (Prestel, Munich, London and New York, 2001).
Passenger Liners Scandinavian Style (Bruce Peter, Carmania Press, London, 2003).
Salute to the Crown (Frank Braynard, Royal Cruise Line / Berlitz Publications, Lausanne, 1988).
The Saga of Norwegian Shipping (Kaare Petersen, Dreyers Forlag, Oslo, 1955).
Trip Out in Southern Europe (G. P. Hamer, London, 1990.)

NOTE
Because the name recurs through several generations, I have tried to avoid confusion by referring to 'the first Fred. Olsen', 'the second Fred. Olsen' and so on. (The name Fred., by the way, is an abbreviation for Fredrik and is always followed by a full stop.) Also, the same ship names tend to crop up again and again in this story. In order to distinguish one vessel from another, I have added a Roman numeral in brackets where this has been necessary: thus *Black Watch (iii)*

1.

The Early Days

In terms of population, Norway is not a big country. Even to-day, little more than 4$^{1}/_{2}$ million people live there. Yet for a century and a half it has been one of the leading shipowning nations in the World, often having the third, fourth or fifth largest fleet.

The national involvement with the sea and ships was partly brought about by geography. Much of the country's interior is mountainous or otherwise almost barren, and the construction of roads and railways has been difficult and sometimes impossible. The coasts are heavily indented by fjords which, while wonderfully attractive, present further obstacles to road-building. So, with a substantial proportion of the population living in coastal settlements, it has been inevitable that ships should form an unusually important part of the national transport system. In addition, for centuries many Norwegians had little alternative but to turn to the sea in order to make a living – large parts of the country are unsuitable for much

The first generation of a famous shipowning family: Fredrik Christian Olsen (1815-75), Andreas Olsen (1826-93) and Petter Olsen (1821-99), who were based in the small village of Hvitsten on what is now Oslofjord. *(Fred.Olsen & Co.)*

in the way of agriculture and, with a lack of coal deposits, Norway was late in participating in the industrial revolution.

For many years it was, in fact, one of the poorest countries in Europe. The sea and fish were its major assets. In the late nineteenth century, as it became possible for better-off foreigners to travel, the tourist industry began to blossom and in the second half of the twentieth-century the discovery of oil and gas below the North Sea gave the economy a further boost. But shipping, and the various businesses which surround it, have always been one of the country's major sources of employment and revenue.

At first, Norwegian ships mainly plied their trade up and down their own coastline. For many years, the national merchant fleet consisted largely of hundreds of small, local vessels, most of which were still sail-powered. As late as 1900, sailing ships amounted to roughly 1 million gross tons while there were only about 500,000 tons of steamships. The cost of switching to steam and the nature of much of their trade meant that Norwegian owners were slower than most in making the transition.

Although, from the seventeenth century onwards, some Norwegian ships carried fish, timber or ice abroad, there was otherwise little reason for them to 'trade foreign'. Theirs was a small country, almost isolated on the north-west corner of Europe, hundreds of miles from the major trade routes. And political circumstances were discouraging. Not only did Norway lack an empire requiring links with the motherland – a major factor in the development of the merchant fleets of some other European nations – but it did not become a fully independent state until Swedish rule finally ended in 1905. Nevertheless, regular routes were established to, for instance, Hamburg, Rotterdam, Antwerp and, very importantly, the British east coast ports. And some Norwegian shipowners saw the opportunities offered by the freeing up of worldwide trade in the second half of the nineteenth century. It was now possible for outsiders to participate in trade to other nations' colonies. By the turn of the century, an energetic new generation of Norwegian owners was going out into the World and competing for business. One of the most notable of these was the second Fred. Olsen (1857-1933).

Some Norwegian shipowners ran regular lines, such as Fred. Olsen's services to the Pacific coast of America, to South America and bringing tomatoes and other fruit to northern Europe from the Mediterranean and the Canary Islands. Many others employed vessels in the bulk trades – tramp ships carrying commodities such as coal and grain wherever the demand existed – and, as the twentieth century progressed, the Norwegians also built up a very modern fleet of diesel-powered tankers. These were to play a brave and crucial rôle in keeping Britain supplied with oil during the Second World War.

For a long time, however, Norwegian owners did not

The enterprising second Fred. Olsen (1857-1933) started with two tiny, wooden sailing vessels but eventually controlled a modern fleet of about 60 steamships and motorships totalling 200,000 gross tons. *(Fred. Olsen & Co.)*

participate greatly in the passenger trades, except on the North Sea routes. This was perhaps surprising since a huge emigration was taking place from their country. Indeed, it has been calculated that the proportion of the Norwegian population who migrated to America during the nineteenth and early twentieth centuries was greater than that of any other European country. Most of these often poor and desperate people travelled in British or Danish ships and it was not until 1913 that a successful Norwegian transatlantic service for large numbers of passengers was established.

The origins of the Fred. Olsen Line.

The Olsen family business can be traced back to 1848. In that year, a young shipmaster called Fredrik Christian Olsen followed the example of many of his kind by going into shipowning on his own account. We shall call him 'the first Fred. Olsen' in order to distinguish him from subsequent members of the family who have borne the same name. His parents, who seem to have had little previous connection with the sea, had quite recently settled in the small village of Hvitsten on the Christianiafjord, the long inlet at the head of which stands the nation's capital. To-day, Christianiafjord is known as Oslofjord. (The Olsens have tended to be very conscious

of their heritage and, nearly 150 years later, their cruise ship *Black Prince (ii)* was, in a pleasingly sentimental gesture, registered at Hvitsten for a while.)

As Mr. Harald Bråthen points out: 'the first Fred. Olsen was one of the ice-carriers, ship's captains in a class of their own, engaged in the difficult and dangerous transport of ice from Norway to Britain and to the Continent.' His earliest vessels were wooden schooners of little more than 50 gross tons. Later ships were slightly bigger barques and brigs which were able even to make Atlantic voyages. Life in sail was never easy and Norwegian owners and sailors had a harder time than most. Much of their country's coastline is inhospitable and conditions in the winter months can be very harsh and dangerous. By the time the first Fred. Olsen died in 1875, 10 of the 22 vessels which he had owned during his lifetime had been wrecked while in his service. Nevertheless, he was clearly a successful shipowner. His brothers, Petter and Andreas, also went into business with small fleets of sailing vessels, starting in 1852 and 1860 respectively. The three brothers' substantial houses can still be seen in Hvitsten.

However, it was Petter's son, the second Fred., actually Thomas Fredrik, who established the Olsen name as one of the most significant in Norwegian shipping. He was a practised seaman who had assumed command of one of his father's vessels at the age of 23. In January, 1886, when he was 28, he was given the management of two of his father's ships, the barques *Skien* and *Bayard (ii)*. Over the next few years, he added others to his fleet, either by purchase or by transfer from his father. By far the biggest of these was the Canadian-built ocean-going full-rigger *Morning Light*. A model of this impressive sailing vessel is to be found in the Fred. Olsen Museum at Hvitsten.

It was not, though, until 1896 that, on behalf of a newly-established company called A/S Bonheur, the second Fred. placed an order with the Nylands shipyard in Christiania for a steamship. Delivered the following year, she was a 1,000-tonner and, recalling one of the vessels with which he had started his shipowning career, he called her *Bayard (iii)*. Since then, it has become a family custom that most of their ships should have names beginning with the letter 'B'. Together with the *Bordeaux*, a second-hand steamer purchased as a stop-gap at about the same time, the *Bayard (iii)* started a regular cargo service between Fredriksstad (later spelt with a single 's'), on the lower reaches of the Christianiafjord, and the English port of Garston, on the Mersey. Other ships and other services across the North Sea followed.

It was in 1899, after the death of his father, that the second Fred. transferred his office from Hvitsten to the capital city, Christiania (sometimes spelt Kristiania and later renamed Oslo). He was now beginning his rapid ascent to become one of his country's most important shipowners. In Oslo, there is even a street named after him, Fred. Olsens Gate. There, Fred. Olsen & Co.'s headquarters are partly accommodated in a picturesque house dating back to 1710 which is notable for its elegant interiors. The family home remained at Hvitsten, however, and for many years whenever an Olsen ship passed by on her way to or from Oslo she would lower her ensign in salute and a flag would be lowered onshore in reply.

The biggest and most notable of the Olsen sailing ships was the Canadian-built full-rigger *Morning Light*. Although the second Fred. Olsen bought his first steamship in 1897 he did not completely forsake sail until 1909. *(Fred.Olsen & Co.)*

Olsen was an early proponent of the motor ship. His second, the *Bayard (iv)* of 1915, was typical of many pioneer diesel-engined vessels in not having a funnel. Mainly used on the South American run, she is seen here at anchor in Torbay. *(Newall-Dunn collection)*

In 1915, the year following the opening of the Panama Canal, the second Fred. Olsen established a cargo service to the West Coast of America and Canada. His steamship *Bravo (i)* was the first Norwegian vessel to pass through the canal. *(Newall-Dunn collection)*

In 1900, the second Fred. was asked to take over the management of the struggling A/S Ganger Rolf (i.e.: the Ganger Rolf Company) which ran a two-ship service from Christiania to Rouen. He succeeded in placing it on a much sounder footing and A/S Ganger Rolf still exists as one of the entities within the present-day Fred. Olsen group although the service to Rouen has long since ceased. Over the next few years, Olsen's business expanded at a heady rate as he built up a network of North Sea services, largely by astute purchases of companies which had got into financial difficulties. In 1901, he bought the Dampskibsselskapet Færder (i.e.: the Færder Steamship Company), an important move because the Færder service from Christiania to Grangemouth, in the heart of industrial Scotland, carried passengers as well as cargo. Then, in 1906, the acquisition of the ships and the business of the old-established but failing Østlandske Lloyd gave him not only a route to Antwerp but also one to Newcastle, thus beginning the Olsen family's long association with the River Tyne. (Suspended during the First World War, the former Færder service to Grangemouth was never reinstated as a passenger line since Newcastle was more conveniently situated for many travellers.) In 1912, the purchase of the Norden Dampskibsselskab brought Olsen a service to Rotterdam.

By the outbreak of war in 1914, the second Fred. Olsen's fleet had grown to over 40 vessels. Most of these were small steamers of 1,500 gross tons or less but Olsen was beginning to look beyond the North Sea and was operating a few larger cargo-carriers. Olsen ships were already carrying cobble-stones to pave the streets of South

American cities when, in 1914, he was invited to join a consortium of leading Norwegian shipowners who were running a regular cargo service to Rio de Janeiro, Santos and Buenos Aires under the name Den Norske Syd Amerika Linje (The Norwegian South America Line). In the following year, he started on his own account a cargo service to the West Coast of America and British Columbia via the Panama Canal. The canal had been opened in 1914 and Olsen's *Bravo (i)* was the first Norwegian vessel to pass through it.

The First World War (1914-18) and afterwards.

Norway remained neutral in the First World War but the country's shipping industry was certainly not immune from its effects. Except for what could be brought from the mines on the remote Arctic island of Spitsbergen, virtually all the country's coal had to be imported from Britain. When, between 1916 and 1917, the British government enforced an embargo on coal sales to Norway, the result was disastrous.

Then, in February, 1917 the German government launched an unrestricted U-Boat (i.e.: submarine) offensive in a zone extending from the Bay of Biscay in the south to the Faroe Islands in the north. Norwegian vessels were carrying 'neutrality markings' – vertical stripes of the national red, white and blue colours painted on a ship's sides together with her name and the word Norge (i.e.: Norway). This did not, though, protect her either from U-Boats or from magnetic mines. In 1916 272,496 gross tons of Norwegian shipping was lost due to war causes; 1917 was a dreadful year with the figure rising to no less than 670,440 tons; and in 1918 it was 189,822. The total tonnage of losses during the entire war amounted to 49.6 per cent of the country's merchant fleet as it had been at the outbreak of hostilities. The Olsen fleet suffered badly: 20 ships and 36 men were lost by enemy action. In addition, three ships were seized by the Germans and one was wrecked.

Scandinavian shipowners had been early in adopting the diesel engine. The World's first ocean-going motorship is generally reckoned to have been the *Selandia* which had been ordered in 1910 by the Østasiatiske Kompagni (East Asiatic Company) of Copenhagen from the Burmeister & Wain shipyard, also in the Danish capital city. She entered service in 1912. Like many motorships in those early years, she was a strange-looking beast without funnels since her engine exhausted up a narrow pipe attached to one of her masts. Fred. Olsen's – and Norway's – first motorship was the *Brazil* of 1914 which, as her name implied, was used in the Norwegian South America Line cargo service. (Credit for ordering her, though, must go to another Norwegian owner who sold her to Olsen during her maiden voyage.) One of the main advantages of those early motor vessels was their fuel economy. In addition, their engines and fuel tanks took up less space than the boilers, engines and coal bunkers of

the steamships and therefore left more room for carrying cargo. Motorships also required smaller crews. On the other hand, they were more expensive to build and they tended at first to be noisy and slow and to vibrate badly. For some years, therefore, they were often considered unsuitable for passenger service.

The *Brazil* came from the Aker shipyard in Oslo harbour. Between 1909 and 1985 the Olsens held a controlling shareholding in this concern and in all it built no less than 53 ships for them.

The Inter-War Years.

The period between the wars was a very difficult one for the shipping industry. In 1919-20 there was a brief boom in the world economy but in many countries, including Britain, this quickly subsided and was followed by years of subdued trade and of protectionism. Then the collapse of the American stock markets in the Wall Street Crash of October, 1929 was the last straw which precipitated not merely a recession but the Great Depression. By 1933, industrial production in the United States had declined by 46.8% and 11,000 of the country's 25,000 banks had failed. Unemployment was reckoned to be running at between 20% and 25% of America's 'working' population. Many other countries, including Britain, Norway and Germany, also suffered badly. It was only in the last years of the 1930s that economic recovery

The Olsens entered the Canary Islands and Mediterranean fruit trades in the 1920s. In this busy scene, photographed in 1949, the good-looking *Bengazi* of 1947 is leaving the West India Docks in London bound for the Mediterranean. *(Laurence Dunn, author's collection)*

Very aptly, the ice-covered *Bonn (ii)* was carrying several penguins as deck cargo, perhaps on their way to a zoo or a circus. In this chilly picture, they are being fed by members of the crew who are no doubt feeling the cold more than are their charges. *(Stefan & Petra Behn collection)*

took hold, helped in some cases by an increase in industrial production due to rearmament in preparation for the war which many now feared was imminent.

Shipowners who in the months immediately following the end of the First World War had bought second-hand tonnage or had ordered new vessels at vastly inflated prices quickly came to regret it. Many did not survive the difficult years which followed. The old, reliable shipping cycle in which Bust followed Boom but was itself inevitably succeeded by another Boom now seemed to be a thing of the past.

Unfavourable conditions notwithstanding, the inter-War period was a time of renewal and expansion for the second Fred. Olsen and his successors. It was necessary to replace the war losses quickly and, despite the high price of newbuildings, Olsens took delivery of ten ships between 1918 and 1920. The business was now conducted through Fred. Olsen & Co., in which the second Fred. took into partnership his son Rudolf and Mr. Johan L. Müller. Later, another son, Fredrik (invariably known as Thomas), came into the firm. (A further son, Petter, had gone into shipowning on his own account some years previously, but he had died at a sadly young age in 1913. His firm continued, however, as part of his father's growing empire.)

Significantly, in the early 1920s Olsens entered the fruit-carrying trades from the Iberian Peninsular, the Mediterranean and the Canary Islands to London and to Continental ports. Due to the perishable nature of their northbound cargoes, ships on these routes needed extra speed and had specially ventilated holds. Olsens made a tentative entry into the trade in 1920 but the following year they took a large stake in the services which the Otto Thoresen company, dating back to 1881, had been running on these routes for some years. Thoresens' Spanish services had been started at the instigation of the Norwegian government, under pressure from the Spaniards who had been concerned that Norwegian exports of stockfish to Catholic Spain needed a good shipping service.

Thoresens had been employing fifteen small ships on these routes, all with names beginning with the letter 'S'. Five of them were new motor vessels, but the cost of building them – particularly three which had been ordered from a shipyard in The Netherlands shortly before the Dutch florin rose sharply in the exchange markets – proved too much for the Thoresen company, thus giving the second Fred. his opportunity. The services were now split into two: those from the Canary Islands were taken over by the Olsens' Bonheur company, while those from the Mediterranean eventually became Den Norske Middelhavslinje (the Norwegian Mediterranean Line), jointly owned by Olsens and Mr. Ole Thoresen. In the 1930s, a further series of smart motor ships entered the fleet. 'Fruiters' were traditionally good-looking vessels and these ships which had Olsen names and funnel markings and, in the case of the later ones, beautiful figureheads, often attracted admiring comment as they made their way through the West India Docks to and from their London berths, latterly at the suitably named Canary Wharf. As was customary with fruit-carriers, they had light-coloured hulls since this helped to lower the temperature in the holds by several degrees.

Also during this period, Olsens expanded their Baltic services; took over a company operating on the short sea route from Norway to German ports; started a service to inland ports on the River Rhine; and, in 1929, commissioned their first tanker. They owned several inter-island steamers in the Canaries; and managed one, and for a time two, colliers belonging to the Norges Statsbaner (Norwegian State Railways) which brought coal from Britain and from Spitsbergen.

OPPOSITE: Life could be hard on board ship. In this view, the small cargo vessel *Bonn (ii)* has encountered wintry conditions at Hamburg. In these circumstances, it was sometimes necessary to chip the ice away in order to prevent the ship from becoming top-heavy. *(Stefan & Petra Behn collection)*

The first Olsen steamship, the *Bayard (iii)*, which entered service across the North Sea between Christiania and Garston, on the River Mersey in 1897. *Bayard* has been one of the most frequently used names in the Olsen fleet. *(Fred. Olsen & Co.)*

The *George Washington* of 1916 was the first of several motor ships built for the second Fred. Olsen's new North Pacific service via the Panama Canal. Here she is seen wearing neutrality markings during the First World War. *(Author's collection)*

The small freighter *Bruin* of 1955 was built by an Aberdeen shipyard for the service between Oslo and North German ports. In some respects, she was a traditional Baltic trader, steam-powered and with her masts situated near the extremities of her hull. *(Author's collection)*

A much more modern short-sea trader was the *Breda (ii)* of 1957, mainly used on the Oslo — Rotterdam route. She was built for the new system of palletised cargo handling and stowage which the young third Fred. Olsen was much involved in developing. *(Newall-Dunn collection)*

The smart *Borgland (iii)* of 1953 was built for the jointly-owned South American service, whose funnel colours she wore. Some of her cargo space was refrigerated to enable her to carry fish on her southbound voyages and meat in the northward direction. *(Newall-Dunn collection)*

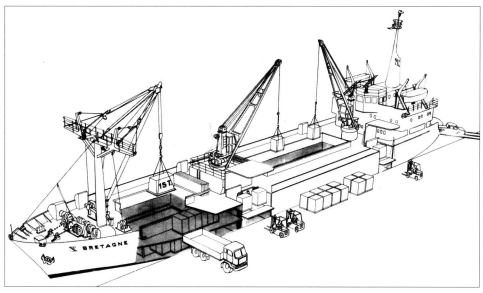

A diagramatic drawing shewing the sophisticated cargo arrangements of the engines-aft *Bretagne (iv)* of 1966, with freight being loaded by deck cranes and by fork-lift trucks which operated through ports in the side of the hull. *(Author's collection)*

The 'reefer' (i.e.: refrigerated cargo ship) *Bentago* of 1983 was built for the Canary Islands fruit trade. Much of her cargo was carried in containers. A strangely idiosyncratic feature was that the Olsen logo protruded beyond the sides of the funnel. *(Newall-Dunn collection)*

The *Borgsten (iii)* of 1964 was a member of the substantial fleet of tankers which Fred. Olsen sold in the early 1970s, correctly anticipating a collapse in the tanker market Note the unusual combined mast and bridge. *(Newall-Dunn collection)*

Some of the Olsen ships on scheduled cargo liner services also had comfortable accommodation for a small number of passengers, usually 12 or less. Here we see the smoke room on the *Bataan* of 1947, which ran in the service to and from the North Pacific. *(John Sutherland collection)*

The smoke room on *Buffalo* and the verandah bar on *Bonanza (i)*, both completed in 1953. Although primarily cargo-carriers, they also catered for just a few leisured passengers who relished a long, quiet voyage to a succession of interesting ports. *(John Sutherland collection)*

2.

Entering the Passenger Trade

As we have seen in the previous chapter, the second Fred. Olsen's first serious venture into the passenger business came in 1901 when he acquired another Christiania-based shipowner, Dampskibsselskapet Færder (the Færder Steamship Company). The Færder service between Christiania and Grangemouth, on the upper reaches of the Firth of Forth, dated back to 1886 and, when Olsen bought it, was being maintained by three ships – the ageing, iron-hulled *Færder* and the more modern, steel-built *Scotland* and *Norway*. These were small vessels of only 1484, 841 and 895 gross tons, respectively.

Although marine engines had by now become much more reliable, the Færder ships, like many of their type, still had provision for raising sail in case of a breakdown. Each of them had accommodation for not much more than 100 passengers. The two younger ships had been fitted with electric lighting, which had gradually been coming into use for some years. (At first, the delicate filaments of the lamps had proved too fragile for rough

conditions at sea but by the turn of the century the problem had largely been solved.)

At the time, the powerful English rival, the Wilson Line, with its network of services from Christiania and other Scandinavian ports to Hull, was carrying many third class 'trans-migrants' who, on reaching Hull, were transferred by train to Liverpool where they were herded on board Atlantic liners for the second stage of their long journey to a new life in America. The Færder ships seem not to have competed for this traffic to any great extent, despite the fact that Grangemouth did have an indirect rail connection with the Atlantic port of Glasgow.

In those days before radar, sailors had to fix their position by taking sights of the sun or stars using a sextant and they were especially vulnerable when weather conditions made this difficult or even impossible. The ships of the Grangemouth service seem to have been particularly unfortunate. In February, 1904, only weeks after being sold to a Danish firm, the *Scotland (i)* was

A painting of the *Scotland (i)* under sail. She was one of the first Olsen passenger ships, joining the fleet when the second Fred. Olsen took over the Færder Line and its passenger and cargo service between Christiania and Grangemouth in 1901. *(Ambrose Greenway collection)*

The *Norway (i)* was another ex-Færder ship. At less than 1,000 gross tons and carrying no more than 100 passengers, in addition to cargo, she was a small vessel, as were the majority of her contemporaries on the North Sea routes in 1901. *(Ambrose Greenway collection)*

wrecked during a snowstorm near Thorshavn in the Faroe Islands. The managers of the original Færder Line had supported 'local' industry by ordering both the *Scotland(i)* and the *Norway(i)* from the Grangemouth Dockyard Co. and it was to that concern that the second Fred. Olsen had turned for a new *Scotland*. Neither he nor they delayed matters and within only four months of the sale of the previous ship her replacement was already being launched. Although slightly larger than her predecessor, the *Scotland (ii)* was very obviously a development of the same design. Unfortunately, she did not last long, running aground in thick fog near Langesund shortly after leaving Christiania in April, 1911. Happily, all her passengers and crew were saved but among the cargo which was lost were the

The *Scotland (iii)* of 1912 was the last passenger-carrying vessel to be built for the service to Grangemouth. Here seen handling cargo, she had only a brief career, being wrecked in 1916.
(Postcard, Ambrose Greenway collection)

A rare picture of *Sterling (i)*, one of the ships of the Østlandske Lloyd which Olsen took over in 1906. He sold her within a few months, replacing her with a more modern vessel. Note her open bridge whose occupants were exposed to the elements. *(Ambrose Greenway collection)*

Norwegian exhibits being sent to the Scottish Exhibition of National History, Art and Industry which was to be held in Kelvingrove Park, Glasgow.

Scotland seems to have been a particularly unlucky name for Olsen ships, since *Scotland (iii)*, the replacement for the vessel lost in 1911, was wrecked on the May Islands in March, 1916 while on her way from Christiania to Leith with a cargo of wood pulp and wooden goods. For some years now, the second Fred. Olsen had been ordering his new ships from Norwegian yards and this one had come from the Nylands Mekaniske Verksted at Christiania in 1912. Two years earlier, in 1910, the Nylands yard had supplied a very similar vessel, the *Norway(ii)*, to replace the former Færder ship of that name, which Olsen had sold to Scottish buyers.

Improving the Newcastle and Antwerp services.

In 1906, when Olsen had taken over the fleet and the routes of the ailing Østlandske Lloyd company, he had immediately been faced with the necessity of replacing several of its ships. Accordingly, he had ordered three new passenger/cargo vessels from the Fredriksstad Mekaniske Verksted, who delivered them in 1907. The most notable of the three was the *Sterling (ii)*, which he placed in the Christiania – Newcastle service, now being advertised as the 'Royal Mail Route'. Here she ran in conjunction with the Middlesbrough-built *Sovereign*, the best of the former Østlandske Lloyd ships. Although still with a gross tonnage of only 1,323, the *Sterling (ii)* was a good, well-equipped ship with her first class passengers travelling in ornately-panelled comfort in the most stable part of the vessel, amidships. Second class passengers were carried at

the stern where the ship's pitching movement was more obvious and where they had to endure the rumble and vibration of the propeller. Third class passengers were housed in stark and crowded quarters in the 'tweendeck. To-day, we would think these conditions intolerable but at the time they were the accepted norm.

The other two new ships which Olsen ordered from the Fredriksstad yard in order to upgrade the former Østlandske Lloyd services were destined for the Christiania – Antwerp route and were given the suitable names of *Brüssel* and *Brabant (i)*. Although marginally slower than the *Sterling (ii)* and distinctly workaday in appearance, they were a definite improvement on the old-fashioned iron-hulled vessels which they displaced.

In 1910, Olsen took delivery of his largest passenger ship yet, the *Paris (i)*, also for the Antwerp service. (Passenger-carrying ships operating on the fairly short North Sea routes were usually far from large, even though they also carried cargo. To place the 1,634 gross ton *Paris (i)* in perspective, it is worth noting that by 1910 the average North Atlantic liner was of perhaps 15,000 gross tons and the largest of them all, the famous *Mauretania*, was an astonishing 31,938 tons. And even larger ships were already being built for that busy and prestigious route. The *Mauretania* had accommodation for 2,300 passengers, including 1,300 in third class, whereas the *Paris (i)* could carry perhaps 80 in all.) Nevertheless, although she was small, she was a sound ship and had a useful cargo capacity. In fact, like the other ships in the Christiania – Antwerp service in those days, she looked very much like a freighter, except that she had an additional pair of lifeboats. As mentioned in the previous chapter, the second Fred. Olsen was now the owner of a

With *Sterling (ii)* of 1907 Olsen improved the former Østlandske Lloyd mail, passenger and cargo service between Christiania (Oslo) and the Tyne. She was the first Olsen passenger steamer to be built in a Norwegian yard. *(Ambrose Greenway collection)*

large stake in the Akers Mekaniske Verksted and he was thus able to place orders with a shipyard under his own control. The *Paris (i)* was the first passenger vessel he received from them. To-day, the shipyard, situated in the very heart of Christiania (now Oslo) harbour, has long since gone and visitors to the Aker Brygge will find that the site is occupied by a marina, residential developments, restaurants and shops.

Lloyd's Register for 1912-13 included two Olsen passenger vessels, the Newcastle steamers *Sovereign* and *Sterling (ii)*, in the still very brief list of ships which had been fitted with the new Marconi wireless telegraphy equipment. As yet, though, none of the fleet is shewn as having refrigeration machinery.

Despite his Aker connection, it was to the Nylands yard that Olsen turned for two more passenger ships for delivery in 1912. One was the Grangemouth service's short-lived *Scotland (iii)*, which we have already met. The other was the somewhat bigger *Bessheim* (1,781 gross tons as against the 1,490 of the *Scotland (iii)*). The *Bessheim* was Olsen's most powerful and fastest passenger ship so far and it was an indication of the growing importance of the Newcastle service that he placed her on that route. The *Sovereign* having been sold, the service could now be maintained by two modern vessels, the *Bessheim* and the *Sterling (ii)*, with one sailing per week in each direction.

One of the pair would depart Newcastle every Friday evening. Each crossing took two days or more, including a call at Arendal, and it will be seen that the ships spent a great deal of their time in port at one end of the route or the other. This was necessary because – unlike many present-day vessels on short-sea routes, much of whose freight is carried on lorries or trailers which are driven on and off through doors in the hull – ships of their generation carried their cargo in holds at either end of the hull, raising and lowering it through hatches in the deck by means of booms and derricks, a laborious process. Many years later, Olsen's grandson, the third Fred., was very active in devising more efficient methods of handling cargo.

Neutral but vulnerable.

The First World War lasted from August, 1914 until November, 1918. Throughout this time, Norway remained neutral, trading with both sides and needing to import food and other supplies from overseas. At first, the Fred. Olsen passenger ships continued to maintain their regular services although, as neutrals, they were unarmed and therefore unable to protect themselves. Warships from both sides often stopped them in order to inspect them for contraband. The Germans, in particular, were infuriated that many Norwegian ships were being chartered to the British and they did not hesitate to seize

In this pre-First World War view, the Antwerp steamer *Paris (i)*, on the left, and the Grangemouth service's *Norway (ii)*, to the right, are in port together. Both had been completed in 1910 and both would be torpedoed in 1917. *(Ambrose Greenway collection)*

The advent of the *Bessheim* in 1912 marked a further improvement of the service to the Tyne, where she is pictured at the Fred. Olsen berth. Note the paddle-driven steam tug lying alongside in this very 'period' picture. *(Postcard, Ambrose Greenway collection)*

A product of the Olsen-controlled Akers shipyard, the four-masted *Paris (ii)* of 1922 is here seen handling cargo in the port of Antwerp, from where some of her passengers will have continued their journey to the French capital by train. *(Postcard, Newall-Dunn collection)*

or sink any vessel they considered to be operating for the enemy. For a time, it was almost impossible for Norwegian shipowners to arrange insurance against war risks but, with the encouragement of the government and the participation of the country's insurance companies, they eventually set up a mutual scheme to provide the necessary cover.

As we saw in the previous chapter, the Norwegian merchant fleet suffered grievous losses and the Fred. Olsen passenger ships on the North Sea were especially vulnerable. The company lost three of them, the *Brabant (i)*, the *Paris (i)* and the *Norway (ii)*, by German torpedoes or mines in the disastrous year of 1917. In addition, as we have seen, the *Scotland (iii)* had been wrecked in 1916. Also in that year, the *Bessheim* had a narrow escape when, in gale force winds, she stranded on a rock at the mouth of the Tyne. Her passengers were rescued thanks to the bravery of the local lifeboatmen and, after a week, it proved possible to refloat her and nurse her to safety. She was repaired and returned to service but soon she and the *Sterling (ii)* were laid up at Christiania and regular passenger sailings more or less ceased.

Post-War reconstruction.

After the Armistice, there could be no question of immediately resuming the passenger service to Grangemouth – both the *Scotland (iii)* and the *Norway (ii)*

had gone and, in fact, the service was never revived for passengers. The routes to Newcastle and to Antwerp, on the other hand, were quickly restarted, with the former being again operated by the *Bessheim* and the *Sterling (ii)*. Unfortunately, the *Sterling (ii)* was wrecked on the Norwegian coast in the Skagerak in March, 1922. There was no loss of life. The Nylands shipyard delivered a similar but slightly larger (1,807 gross tons) replacement, the *Blenheim (i)*, in the following year. Despite competition from the bigger steamers of the Wilson Line (which had now become part of the influential group of British shipping companies controlled by Sir John Ellerman), the Fred. Olsen service to Newcastle would seem to have prospered and eventually was increased from one to two sailings per week in each direction during the summer months, partly in order to take advantage of the growing tourist trade.

At first, the service to Antwerp was maintained single-handedly by the *Brüssel* but in 1922 the Akers yard delivered two new ships whose rôle as cargo- as well as passenger-carriers was emphasised by their having no less than four masts, each with cargo gear attached. The memory of the lost *Paris (i)* was perpetuated by a new *Paris (ii)* and the second ship was called *Biarritz*. As these names implied, the Antwerp route was not only patronised by passengers travelling between Norway and Belgium but, with train connections, was also a convenient way of

Blenheim (i) of 1923 was a younger but very similar sister and running-mate to the pre-First World War *Bessheim* on the route to the Tyne. As the 1920s and 1930s progressed, competition on the North Sea increased sharply. *(Postcard, Bruce Peter collection)*

going further south, into France. At Antwerp, buses transferred passengers and their luggage between the ship and the station.

A further passenger vessel was acquired by an Olsen subsidiary during this period and should not be forgotten although, with a gross tonnage of only 191, she was tiny and might be best described as a steamboat rather than a ship. Called the *Oscarsborg 1*, she had started life in 1904 as the Swedish *Styrsö 1* but had been purchased by a local Oslo company for use as a *fjordbåt* (fjord boat) in 1911. They ran her in regular service around the inner Oslofjord carrying passengers and a certain amount of light cargo.

The Olsens bought her in 1919. Still under the management of her previous owners but wearing the Olsen funnel colours, she now provided a link between Hvitsten and Oslo (or rather, Christiana as it was then known), also calling at other fjord communities. It would seem that she was bought not only with the intention of providing a useful public service but also for the convenience of the Olsen family. This quaint, long-lived little boat remained in their service until 1953 and was then sold to other owners who re-engined her and converted her into a cargo-carrier.

A very different Fred. Olsen passenger-carrier, the tiny 1911-built *Oscarsborg 1*, sometimes known locally as the *Borgen*, was a familiar sight around the Oslofjord. Her main purpose was to provide a link between the Olsens' home village of Hvitsten and Oslo. *(Fred. Olsen & Co.)*

3.

A New Era

Difficult times though they were in most areas of the shipping industry, the 1920s and the early 1930s saw many developments and improvements. This was certainly the case on the North Sea routes. Bigger and better vessels came onto the scene and, in particular, Scandinavian owners were now sufficiently confident of the motor ship to introduce examples into their passenger services where, with newly-developed high-speed engines, they proved to be extremely successful.

The first of these North Sea motorliners was the *Parkeston* which the DFDS company of Copenhagen placed in service between Esbjerg and Harwich in October, 1925. But the second Fred. Olsen was not far behind and took delivery of the motor-powered *Brabant (iii)* for his Antwerp service in March, 1926. Hitherto, most of his ships had been driven by traditional triple-expansion steam engines with boilers heated by coal-fired furnaces. But, as we have already seen in an earlier chapter, he had been operating motor ships on his transatlantic cargo routes since 1915. Also, since 1918 he had added several small motor freighters to his North Sea

and Mediterranean cargo fleets. (Open to new developments, in 1920 he had also commissioned a very early example of a steamship driven by turbo-electric machinery. He did not repeat the experiment.) Now, the new *Brabant (iii)* was his first motor-driven passenger liner and she attracted a great deal of attention. A product of the Aker yard, she had a gross tonnage of 2,335 and was Olsen's biggest passenger ship so far. Akers had themselves built her two 6-cylinder diesel engines under licence from the Danish pioneers Burmeister & Wain.

Although the *Brabant (iii)* was technically a very modern ship, photographs shew that her passenger accommodation must already have seemed somewhat old-fashioned. She had accommodation for up to 70 first class passengers amidships and could carry 30 third class travellers in less comfortable quarters at the stern. She also had space for 2,500 tons of cargo in two substantial holds. She was a more modern-looking ship than her predecessors and instead of their traditional, deeply curved counter sterns, she had one of the newly-fashionable cruiser sterns which were more easily constructed and

The first of a notable new generation of Olsen passenger ships, the motorliner *Brabant (iii)* of 1926 is seen at Antwerp on the 18 July, 1934. At this stage, she still had no funnel but one was fitted three years later when she was thoroughly modernised. *(Ambrose Greenway collection)*

The 70-seat first class dining room on *Brabant (iii)* had a very traditional look, with handsome wooden panelling and with long tables and swivel chairs firmly fixed to the deck in case the North Sea was in a turbulent mood. *(Author's collection)*

maintained. The funnel-less style of the early motor vessels had not found favour in some quarters, especially with crews who often felt that it gave their ships an embarrassingly emasculated look, and many owners were now specifying that their new motor vessels should be fitted with funnels. At first, these were often quite vestigial – small, upright tubes topped with a cowl – but, later, more substantial funnels came into fashion on motor ships. Olsen, however, held firm and, as built, the *Brabant (iii)* had no funnel. Her engines exhausted through two slender pipes attached to the second of her three masts. However, in 1937 she was given a far-reaching refit from which she emerged with just two masts and a conventional short funnel of the type which was becoming customary on motor ships.

The death of the second Fred. Olsen.

The Olsen companies were not unscathed by the Great Depression of the early 1930s. The second Fred. Olsen's policy of consistently up-dating his fleet by placing new orders, often with the Aker yard, was slowed down and at one stage had to be briefly abandoned. Nevertheless, at a time when many good ships were being taken out of service and 'laid up', or even scrapped, the Olsens managed to keep almost all their fleet running. Unlike many other well-known shipowners, they survived.

On the 29th January, 1933, the second Fred. Olsen died at the age of 76. Inevitably, this was a blow to the firm, particularly as it came at such a difficult time. He had achieved so much, starting in a very small way but becoming one of the most important shipowners in a

A somewhat congested deck scene on *Brabant (iii)* with the cargo gear, large ventilators and wooden lifeboats which were all typical of traditional ship design. Mechanically and structurally, however, *Brabant (iii)* was an extremely modern ship. *(Author's collection)*

Brabant (iii) after her modernisation in 1937, intended to make her compatible with the new *Bretagne (iii)* on the Oslo — Antwerp route. She has now been endowed with a funnel and it carries the new Fred. Olsen colours. *(Alex Duncan, author's collection)*

Bali, an opportunist purchase by Olsens in the mid-1930s, was a coal-fired steamer. Very evidently, the tug at her stern was also a coal-burner. In the difficult years after the Second World War, *Bali* rendered very useful service in a much-depleted fleet. *(Newall-Dunn collection)*

Olsen involvement in the newly emerging commercial airline business began in 1933 when they set up DNL (The Norwegian Aviation Company), one of the predecessors of the later pan-Scandinavian line, SAS. Here is one of DNL's Junker JU52 flying boats. *(Fred.Olsen & Co.)*

country which was certainly not short of vigorous entrepreneurs. At the time of his death, the London shipping newspaper *Lloyd's List* noted that he had controlled 'a fleet of about 60 ships with a total tonnage of 200,000 tons'. Much later, in a history of Norwegian shipping published in 1955, he was singled out, along with A. F. Klaveness and Morten Wilhelmsen, as having been one of the men who had succeeded in creating large firms in this very competitive industry.

Fred. Olsen & Co. and its associated companies were now controlled by his sons Rudolf (who had gained the prestigious rank of Consul General) and Thomas. The Great Depression of the 1930s, for all its adverse effects on their trade, did eventually give them the opportunity to acquire a useful passenger-carrying addition to the hitherto mainly cargo service on the Oslo – Rotterdam route which often included calls at Kristiansand and, if cargo was on offer, various small southern Norwegian 'outports'. The *Alnwick* had been completed as lately as 1928 (not 1929 as is sometimes stated) for the Tyne-Tees Steam Shipping Company by Swan, Hunter & Wigham Richardson at their famous Neptune yard at Low Walker, Newcastle upon Tyne. Latterly, she had been employed in the Tyne-Tees company's Newcastle to London service. But times were hard and competition from motor coaches and lorries was increasingly affecting carryings on this coastal route, where some of her most frequent passengers were said to be football fans travelling south when Newcastle United were playing London teams. She had been quickly taken out of service and in December, 1935 she was sold to one of the Fred. Olsen companies, who gave her the rather exotic name of *Bali*. After being refurbished at Oslo, the 1,428 gross ton ship entered service in April, 1936.

She must have been something of a bargain since Olsens had only paid about £35,000 for her. Although she had the reputation of being a 'wet ship' (liable to ship water over her foredeck in heavy seas), she was well-built and served Olsens faithfully until 1952. In a sense, though, she represented a backward step for them, since she was powered by old-fashioned triple-expansion steam engines and the furnaces which heated her boilers were coal-fired. She could carry 1,400 tons of cargo but like the other ships in Olsens' North Sea services in those days, she had a rather limited passenger capacity – in her case it was about 100 in two classes. Female passengers were allowed to travel in the cheaper accommodation, which was still known as third class, whereas on the *Biarritz*, now her companion on the Rotterdam route, the very communal facilities were not considered suitable for this to be permitted.

Momentum regained.

During the latter half of the 1930s, the Olsen brothers were able to restore some of the momentum which had been lost during the Great Depression. They were, for instance, quick to realise that although the development of air travel threatened possible competition for their passenger shipping services it could also present opportunities. In fact, their father had already considered entering the airline business as early as 1926-27 but had concluded that it was too soon to make a move. In 1933, however, his sons were involved in setting up Det Norske Luftfartsselskap (The Norwegian Aviation Company), often referred to as DNL. Soon, the Bergen Line and several other shipowners joined them in this enterprise. After suspending services during the War, DNL became, in August 1948, one of the components of the new Scandinavian Airways System (SAS), in which the Olsens were major shareholders for the next 50 years. (Their involvement in aviation also included the formation of their own airline, Fred. Olsens Flyselskap, which operated in the charter market and often carried crews to and from ships in various parts of the World, both for themselves

A later Fred. Olsen 'plane: one of the ubiquitous Douglas Dakota DC3s, willing workhorses from America which played a crucial role in the development of many well-known airlines in the years after the Second World War. *(Fred.Olsen & Co.)*

and for other owners, and later became a significant cargo-carrier. For a time, they were also leading shareholders in the Norwegian regional airline Widerøe and, until 2005, in Sterling Airways, a Danish company. They have now disposed of all their aviation interests.)

In any case, in the mid- and late 1930s shipping was still their main business and they introduced several notable new vessels into their fleet of 'fruiters'. The Canary Islands part of the fruit trade was not without its problems, however. Following the election of a Republican government in Spain and the fall of the monarchy in April, 1931 and then the outbreak of the vicious Spanish Civil War in 1936 (which did not directly affect the Canaries too much but nevertheless disrupted trade quite seriously), shipments of produce from the islands were greatly reduced.

In 1937 – 38, the Aker yard delivered three notable new ships which represented an upward step-change in the Olsen North Sea passenger business. The weekly service between Oslo and Antwerp now received the handsome *Bretagne (iii)* of 3,285 gross tons. Externally, she was a sleek, modern-looking vessel with a long, raked, flush-decked bow, a low funnel and a cruiser stern. As will be seen in the next chapter, Olsens were now reviving the old custom of adorning the bows of their ships with figureheads and this undoubtedly added to the allure of this attractive little liner. She also benefited from wearing the new livery which the company had recently adopted. For years, the funnels on Olsen ships had been painted black with a red band bearing the family's flag on either side. Now they had become buff-yellow, but still adorned with the flag which was depicted in a rather larger form. That flag, white with its swallow tail and with a blue dot and a diagonal blue bar, had first been flown by the second Fred. Olsen on his racing yacht in the 1890s but was to become one of the best known in Europe.

The *Bretagne (iii)* was a faster ship than the Olsens' previous passenger-carriers – her powerful 9-cylinder Burmeister & Wain-type diesel engine, which drove a single screw, gave her a service speed of 16 knots as against her older fleetmates' 13 knots. She could carry 88 first class passengers, mainly in single-berth cabins, together with 26 in second class and 34 in third. Her first class interiors were particularly fine, being the work of Arnstein Arneberg, perhaps the most notable Norwegian architect of the day, and Andre Peters. This marked the beginning of a productive association between Olsens and Arneberg and it was fitting that at Oslo the Olsen liners should dock within sight of Arneberg's greatest work, the magnificent City Hall, built between 1931 and 1951 and famous as the venue for the presentation of the Nobel Peace Prize. It was with the introduction of the *Bretagne (iii)*, that the *Brabant (iii)* was so comprehensively refitted in order to make her more compatible with her new running-mate.

The other two new ships, introduced slightly later, were both intended for the route between Oslo and Newcastle. Although there was no direct competition to this service, it was becoming urgently necessary to upgrade it. The Swedish Lloyd company's extremely popular 4,000-ton, 17½ knot turbine steamers *Suecia* and *Britannia* had been running between Gothenburg and London since 1929; and the Bergen Line's unsteady but stylish 5,000-ton motor ship *Venus* had been maintaining a service speed of 19 knots between Bergen and Newcastle since 1931. Good rail connections linking Oslo with both Gothenburg and Bergen enabled these ships to tempt passengers away from the older, smaller and much slower Olsen steamers *Bessheim* and *Blenheim (i)*. (Gothenburg was only six and a half hours away from Oslo by train.) To add to the seriousness of the situation, the Bergen company was planning a magnificent new running-mate for the *Venus* – the beautiful, Italian-built *Vega* which eventually emerged in 1938 with a gross tonnage of 7,000 and a service speed of 20 knots. And although Ellerman's Wilson Line had hardly updated its passenger fleet since the First World War, its green-hulled Oslo – Hull ships still provided considerable competition.

The Olsen brothers' reply came in 1938 as part of a massive modernisation programme on which they had embarked two years earlier. Between 1936 and the outbreak of the Second World War, they introduced no fewer than eleven new ships, mainly freighters. As a result of this huge investment, they provided the Aker yard, who built ten of them, with a sustained period of busy employment. The programme included two of the most notable passenger ships yet to sail on the North Sea routes. Olsens' strong British connection was recognised by the historic names they gave these new liners, *Black Prince (i)* and *Black Watch (i)*. The importance of these 5,035-ton motorships had been recognised by Royal patronage, when the first of the pair was launched from the Aker yard by Crown Princess Martha on the 22nd December, 1937. (These ships are sometimes said to have been the largest yet built in Norway but, in fact, the Aker yard had in 1932 completed a bigger vessel, the motor freighter *Vivi*, for other owners.)

Not only did the pair have elegantly up-to-date exteriors, as Stephen Card demonstrates so beautifully in his painting on the dust jacket of this book, but their interiors, again designed by Arnstein Arneberg and Andre Peters, combined modernity with a very Norwegian atmosphere, as can be seen in the accompanying illustrations. In particular, local craftsmen provided some notable artworks. In his book *Passenger Liners Scandinavian Style*, Bruce Peter comments that the ships 'were particularly inventively planned. For example, the main dining saloon could be split into a series of smaller rooms using retractable bulkheads and the galley was located on the deck below with an interconnecting lift.' In an era when many people had become obsessed with exercise and fresh air, there was notably more open deck space than had hitherto been customary. And first class passengers could enjoy a 'Finnish vapour bath' (i.e.: a sauna), which would have been unthinkable on North Sea ships of a previous generation. For the more frivolously inclined, *Lloyd's List* noted that music for dancing could be provided by a radio receiver. There were also 'phone boxes 'with full ship and shore telephone facilities'. These new mini-liners had a substantially larger passenger capacity than their predecessors - 185 in first class and 65 in second. There was also accommodation for postal staff since Olsens had long had a contract to carry the mails.

Each sister had two 9-cylinder diesel engines and could maintain a speed of 18 knots. The necessarily slow passage up the Oslofjord meant that the voyage between the Tyne and Oslo took 32 hours, still no match for the

The *Bretagne (iii)*, introduced onto the Antwerp route in 1937, shews off her modern cruiser stern. The famous Norwegian architect Arnstein Arneberg was involved in the design of her first class interiors and later received several other commissions from Olsens. *(Postcard, author's collection)*

In 1938, the service to the Tyne was revitalised by the arrival of two fine new motorliners, Olsens' biggest and fastest yet. *Black Prince (i)*, seen here, and *Black Watch (i)* were acknowledged to be two of the best furnished, most stylish ships on the North Sea *(Newall-Dunn collection)*

Bergen Line opposition, but for passengers disembarking during the intermediate call at Kristiansand (which now had a good rail link with Oslo and had replaced Arendal, or occasionally Horten, in the schedule) the voyage time was 23 hours, enabling Olsens to claim 'the shortest open sea crossing'. In any case, they could now offer their passengers an unprecedented degree of comfort and style. In the peak summer season, the fare for a one-way voyage between Newcastle and Oslo was £5 10s. 0d. (£5.50) in first class and £3 15s. 0d. (£3.75) in second class. A brochure stated: 'these prices include victualling on board, landing and embarkation dues in Newcastle and tips on board.' To boost passenger traffic in the slack winter months, the line offered inclusive holidays at several ski resorts. In May, 1938, in anticipation of the advent of *Black Prince (i)* the following month, the by now outdated steamship *Bessheim* was laid up at Oslo.

To coincide with the introduction of the new liners, a dedicated terminal was built for them at the Newcastle end of the route, at the Tyne Commission Quay at North Shields, a couple of miles downstream from the old berth. The Bergen Line had been established there since 1928 and there was a rail link with Newcastle Central Station.

1938 was, in fact, an *annus mirabilis* for Norwegian passenger shipping, with four outstanding liners entering service: the Olsen twins, the Bergen Line's *Vega* and the 18,000-ton *Oslofjord* of the Norwegian America Line. Tragically, they were to have only the briefest of lives, all four being sunk during the War. On learning of the loss of *Black Prince (i)*, *Lloyd's List* described her as 'one of the outstanding products of immediate pre-war naval architecture in Europe and a credit to her builders and designers'.

The New **FRED. OLSEN** Luxury Liner

The **Black Prince**

5,200 TONS   18 KNOTS

commences regular express sailings between

NEWCASTLE *and* **NORWAY**

ON SATURDAY, MAY 21st

Luxurious cabins with real beds, hot and cold wash-hand basins and controlled ventilation: fresh water, sea water and Turkish baths: spacious lounge tastefully decorated and furnished: comfortable smoke room and lounge with cocktail bar: magnificent restaurant with first-class cuisine and service: extensive prom- | enade and sun decks: open and closed verandas: day and night radio tele-phone and telegraph service: many other outstanding features.

Sailing times, cabin reservations, etc., from your Travel Agent or from Norwegian State Railways, 51. Norway House, Cockspur Street, London, S.W.1.

Open sea passage 23 hours

THE MOST MODERN LUXURY LINER IN THE NORTH SEA

A preliminary advertisement announcing the introduction of the new *Black Prince (i)* in 1938. She and her sister made a huge impression but, unfortunately, the advent of the Second World War meant that they had less than two years in commercial service. *(Author's collection)*

4.
A Tradition Revived

Over the years, the Olsens have been very conscious of their shipping heritage. Never has this been more evident than in their revival in the 1930s of the attractive old tradition of decorating ships' bows, often with figureheads – sculptures of human figures.

This custom had faded out in the latter years of the nineteenth century when steamships had ceased to use sails, except sometimes in emergencies, and had therefore no longer needed bowsprits. Furthermore, modern methods of shipbuilding at the time had prompted the introduction of the bar stem, in which the plating of the hull was attached to a massive bar of iron or steel to form a sharply pointed, vertical bow on which a figurehead would have sat awkwardly. Occasionally, it is true, some particularly prestigious vessel would still be given a bow decoration. Perhaps most notably, the huge German transatlantic liner *Imperator* of 1913 was made even

One of the more traditionally styled figureheads on the Olsen ships was that on the bow of the Oslo — Antwerp liner *Bretagne (iii)*. *(Newall-Dunn collection)*

It was not only the passenger ships which were given figureheads. Here is Sigurd Nome's sculpture for the *Bonanza (i)*, a freighter on the North Pacific route. *(Newall-Dunn collection)*

longer and more imposing by the addition of a gigantic bronze eagle on her prow. This fearsome bird was partly demolished by an Atlantic storm the following year and its remains were hastily removed.

In the mid-1930s, however, new building techniques saw ships being given much more raked and rounded bows and two Norwegian firms in particular – Fred. Olsen and Thor Dahl – chose to adorn them with decorative sculptures. From 1936, with the introduction of the 'fruiter' *Bayard (v)*, until 1970, almost every Fred. Olsen vessel – cargo ships as well as passengers liners – had one. Distinguished sculptors were commissioned to produce these works of art, which were often brightly and attractively coloured. In a few cases, however, it was impracticable to attach a sculpture to the front of a ship. Several post-War tankers, for instance, were intended to make frequent passages through the Suez Canal, where they would be required to sling a large lamp over the bow. Free-standing decorations would have got in the way but, nothing daunted, the Olsens commissioned well-known artists to produce abstract two-dimensional designs instead. Usually, these were painted onto the bow and the blocks of colour were outlined with spot welding so

One of the best-known bows in the cruise business: that of _Black Prince (ii)_ with her beautiful figurehead by Kjell Rasmussen.
(Newall-Dunn collection)

placed over the entrance to what was then the company's passenger office in Regent Street, London.

To-day, new Olsen ships are no longer given these decorations but examples can still be seen in various places on board the present cruise ships. _Black Prince (ii)_ still proudly carries Kjell Rasmussen's figure of the Norwegian ballerina Anne Borg on her bow, while these days there is on her upper deck the sculpture which once adorned the stem of the 'fruiter' _Balblom_. The other ships of the present Fred. Olsen Cruise Lines fleet also have examples from former Olsen vessels either as part of their interior décor or as features on their open decks. The _Boudicca_, for instance, has a bronze nude from the _Baldrian_ of 1947 on one of her after decks. In addition, no less than 31 bow decorations are displayed in a sort of 'figurehead farm' in the grounds at Hvitsten; and others are at the company offices in Oslo, on the third Fred. Olsen's estates in Scotland and Norway and in the grounds of Jardin Tecina, the hotel which Olsens own on the island of La Gomera. The imposing figure from the South America Line _Bolivar_ is particularly interesting as it was salvaged from the ship after she was wrecked on the return leg of her maiden voyage in 1947. Another particularly spectacular sculpture is that from _Black Prince (i)_ which can now be seen at the Dover Cruise Terminal – very suitably, since Fred. Olsen cruise ships are frequent callers there.

The launch of the small freighter _Bastant_ on the 3rd December, 1963. Her bow is decorated by an elaborate abstract design. _(Newall-Dunn collection)_

that when the ships were repainted the decoration could be restored exactly as it had been.

Some other owners attached small badges to the bows of their ships but only a few followed Olsens' lead and commissioned full-scale sculptures. The Polish liners _Pilsudski_ and _Batory_ of 1935 and 1936 had rare examples, as, at first, did the Norwegian America Line's _Oslofjord_ of 1949 and _Bergensfjord_ of 1956. But it was the Olsen ships, above all, which became famous for this feature. Was the expense justified in a harsh commercial world? Olsens obviously thought so.

Particularly notable were the bow decorations on the tragically short-lived _Black Prince (i)_ and _Black Watch (i)_ of 1938. The former was the armoured figure of the Black Prince himself and was the work of Emil Lie, while the latter represented an officer of the Black Watch Regiment in full dress uniform. This was by Ørnulf Bast, who produced a number of notable works of art which adorned the bows of Fred. Olsen ships. His brightly coloured Black Watch figure was seemingly lost when the ship was sunk in 1945 but when the damaged hulk was raised in 1963 her bow decoration was found to be intact 'encrusted with barnacles but with some of its original paintwork remaining'. It was restored and for a time was

Emil Lie's fine figurehead for _Black Prince (i)_ can now be seen at the Dover Cruise Terminal, these days the starting point of many Fred. Olsen voyages. *(John Sutherland)*

This colourful figurehead by Ørnulf Bast was rescued from the wreck of the war victim _Black Watch (i)_ and, suitably, is now preserved on the Olsen estate in Scotland. *(John Sutherland)*

Figureheads from old Olsen vessels now form part of the décor on the present generation of cruise ships. This one from the *Baldrian* is on the after deck of the *Boudicca*. *(John Sutherland)*

Another figurehead rescued from an ill-fated Olsen ship, in this case the South American Line freighter *Bolivar*, is now on view at Jardin Tecina on the island of La Gomera. *(John Sutherland)*

Many former bow decorations can also be seen in the Olsen family's home village of Hvitsten, some miles out of Oslo. This one by Alfred Seland came from the cargo ship *Bysanz*. *(John Sutherland)*

This particularly exotic figurehead, now to be seen at Jardin Tecina on La Gomera, once decorated the bow of *Bencomo (i)*, a Canary Islands 'fruiter'. *(John Sutherland)*

One of several works by Ørnulf Bast which have decorated the bows of Olsen ships, this bright figure from the North Pacific cargo liner *Bataan* is now preserved at Hvitsten. *(John Sutherland)*

After years of facing the violence of North Sea waves, Per Hurum's bow shield from *Braemar (i)* now forms part of the décor in the restful Braemar Lounge on *Black Watch (iii)*. *(John Sutherland)*

5.

Second World War

German forces invaded Poland on the 1st September, 1939 and two days later Britain and France declared war. The Norwegians hoped that, as in the First World War, they would be able to remain neutral and that their country would be inviolate. It was not to be. The Germans were eyeing Norwegian ports from which they could mount attacks on British shipping in the North Atlantic and they needed Swedish iron ore, which had to be brought by rail across Norway before being shipped through the port of Narvik.

Nevertheless, for a few months all seemed well and Norway was left alone. As in the First World War, the Norwegian merchant shipping fleet became even more important to the nation's well-being, both in order to bring in supplies of oil, coal and other necessities and as a source of foreign exchange earnings. Norwegian liner shipping companies tried to maintain their regular pre-War cargo services, while many owners of tramps and tankers chartered them either to the still-neutral Americans or to the British. Once again, the Norwegians had to tread a careful line, trading with one of the belligerent powers while attempting to maintain their neutrality. In fact, despite the neutrality markings painted on the sides of their hulls, Norwegian ships were at considerable risk, as were the men who sailed them.

The realities of war were brought home to everyone connected with the Fred. Olsen fleet when, on the first day of the conflict, their cargo liner *Knute Nelson*, employed in the service to the American West Coast, hastened to the rescue of survivors from the torpedoed Donaldson Line passenger ship *Athenia*. The Olsen vessel was able to save 449 of them, whom she landed at the Irish port of Galway two days later. She must have been very crowded and short of food and water. Tragically, in the dark and in a heavy swell, a lifeboat from the *Athenia* had come into contact with one of the *Knute Nelson*'s propellers during the rescue and was ripped apart. 47 of its occupants were killed.

The big motor freighter *Knute Nelson* picked up 449 survivors from the torpedoed British liner *Athenia* on the 3rd September, 1939, the very first day of the Second World War. She was herself torpedoed and sunk in 1944. *(Author's collection)*

Even before the invasion of Norway in April, 1940, Olsen ships and men were at risk. *Segovia*, **one of the former Thoresen 'fruiters', disappeared without trace in January, 1940. It is thought that she had been torpedoed.** *(Newall-Dunn collection)*

Tragedy struck again in the early weeks of 1940. First, the small 'fruiter' *Segovia* disappeared without trace on the 21st January and was presumed to have been torpedoed. 23 lives were lost. Then, only four days later, the *Biarritz* hit a mine while en route from Antwerp to Oslo and sank within minutes. Recently reactivated after a period in lay-up, she had been carrying 58 passengers and crew, of whom only 21 survived. On the 28th March, the freighter *Burgos (i)* was mined off the coast of Norfolk while on her way from Bergen to London. Fortunately, on this occasion there were no fatal casualties.

The *Black Prince (i)* and *Black Watch (i)* had been laid up at Oslo – insurance against war risks for such new and valuable vessels would have been too expensive, even if it could have been secured. In April, 1940, they were transferred to the Åsefjord, near Trondheim. For a time, there was an attempt to maintain some sailings to the Tyne using other, older ships. Like the unfortunate *Biarritz*, the laid-up *Bessheim* had been brought back into service and, joining British convoys, she made several voyages on the route.

Invasion.

Norway's uneasy neutrality was short-lived. In the early hours of the 9th April, 1940, under cover of darkness which was hardly dissipated by an almost new moon, German forces came ashore at Narvik, Trondheim, Bergen and Egersund and in the Kristiansand/Arendal area. Warships also entered the Oslofjord but were repulsed by the shore batteries which guarded the narrows about 10 miles south of Oslo. Later that day, however, the capital was captured by paratroopers and by forces landed by transport planes which flew in low over the city.

Almost at a stroke, the Germans had effectively gained control of much of the southern part of the country and King Haakon and the government had been forced to withdraw to the north. By the 9th June, despite British and Allied landings, the whole of the country was, nominally at least, under German occupation. The King and a government-in-exile had been taken to safety in Britain by the Royal Navy cruiser H.M.S. *Devonshire*.

With his wife and young son, the third Fred., Thomas Olsen had made his way to Ålesund. He carried with him a letter, dated the 29th April, from the Norwegian government authorising him to 'bring into safety abroad or in Northern Norway all vessels and supplies of any kind from Møre- and Romsdal county. All military and civilian authorities are asked to support Mr. Thomas Olsen in every way in his work. He has an unlimited right to requisition.' By the 1st May, with the Germans advancing, it became necessary to leave and the Olsens boarded a British warship, H.M.S. *Somali*. She was also carrying a contingent of Royal Marines and some other Norwegians to safety. Many years later, the third Fred. Olsen wrote a vivid account of the voyage. It can be seen, accompanying a photograph in the Braemar Room on *Black Watch (iii)*. Desperate and dangerous though the situation was, it was all an adventure for a young boy:

'The captain wasted no time going for Scapa Flow; the bow spray went over the ship, landing on the after deck, leaving the midship section dry. The marines hung in their hammocks in all the gangways and to my surprise many were seasick. I was taken on a grand tour by Lieut. Commander Maurice Macmullen and on the bridge Captain Nicholson gave me a round candy so large that it filled my mouth to the point of choking. It was great fun, at least for me. On arrival in Scapa Flow, I rode astride a torpedo-tube and saw a large part of the home fleet at anchor. By nightfall we were alongside a pier and to our surprise mistaken for German paratroopers...... Realising the misunderstanding, the Lord Mayor and his wife gracefully let my mother and father have their guest room and I slept on the flower printed sofa in the living room. The next day we left for Thurso on a tugboat. I was invited onto the Bridge and as there was a small hatch through which I could see my father below, I started to tell him of the naval ships in port. In no uncertain terms, he quickly told me to shut up, having understood perfectly why he was not on the bridge. We should have changed places, he had no idea of the ships and I knew *Jane's Fighting Ships* by heart.'

Back home in Hvitsten, one of the company's employees took up residence in the family house – if it had been left unoccupied, it would have been seized by the Germans. Some time after they landed in Britain, Thomas Olsen and his family made their way to America, where they settled in Waterbury, Connecticut. From there, he continued his business activities. It was while he was there that he met the owners of the Waterbury Clock & Watch Company and began the involvement which led to the family's connection with Timex Watches. His brother Rudolf, meanwhile, remained in Oslo to 'mind the shop' there.

Norwegian ships which were in the ports captured at the time of the invasion (or which happened to be in German or occupied Danish ports) were quickly taken under German control. Some ships attempted to escape the enemy's northward advance, usually trying to make for British ports. Many Norwegian vessels were, of course, scattered elsewhere in the World and their captains briefly faced a difficult dilemma as to what they should do. After a few days, the Norwegian government, retreating up-country, decreed that all these ships were to be requisitioned. An organisation called the Norwegian Shipping & Trade Mission (commonly known by its telegraphic address, Nortraship) had already been established in London by the Norwegian Embassy there and by representatives of Norwegian shipowners and it took over the management of that part of the merchant fleet which had not fallen under German control. These vessels would still sail under the Norwegian flag and with Norwegian crews. Of ships over 500 gross tons, no less than 881 came under Nortraship's auspices, as against 273 which were effectively under German control. Eventually, Nortraship was running about 4 million tons of shipping and was sometimes claimed to be 'the biggest shipowner in the World'

Inevitably, so vast and hastily constructed an organisation had its problems. There were frictions between the London office and the one which was later established in New York; and some shipowners, including Thomas Olsen, were not entirely happy about the way Nortraship was being run. Nevertheless, the Norwegian merchant fleet performed heroically in the Allied cause and for a time well over a third of the oil coming into Britain was being carried, at huge risk, by Norwegian tankers.

When the War began in September, 1939, the Fred. Olsen companies had a fine fleet of 57 vessels, of which eleven were three years old or less. By the end of hostilities, 28 of them had been lost, together with 189 officers and men. More happily, three Olsen ships, the *Bomma (ii)*, *Bra-Kar(iii)* and *San Andres*, were members of the contingent of five small vessels which in June, 1940 made a risky but successful voyage across the Atlantic, taking Norway's gold reserves from Britain to safety in the United States.

Also in January, 1940, the passenger steamer *Biarritz*, which had been brought back into service on the Antwerp route, hit a mine and sank almost immediately. Although other ships came to the rescue, 37 lives were lost. (*Fred. Olsen & Co.*)

Passenger ships at war.

Almost all the Fred. Olsen cargo ships came under the control of Nortraship. Circumstances dictated, however, that the passenger fleet could not be available to serve the Allied cause. As we have seen, the *Biarritz* had already been lost and the *Black Prince (i)* and *Black Watch (i)* had been laid up by the time the Germans marched in on the 9th April, 1940. The *Blenheim (i)* was tied up in Oslo on that day and the others were lying idle in various ports in the Oslofjord. Before long, all of them had been taken over and pressed into service by the German authorities who now ruled the country.

In May, the *Black Prince (i)* was seized by the Germans. From August, 1940 until March, 1941, they used her as an accommodation ship for the Luftwaffe (the German air force) at Oslo. She was then handed over to the Kriegsmarine (navy), who utilised her as a depôt ship for U-Boats and their crews, initially at Oslo and then at Danzig. Presumably because her name was so very English, it was later changed to *Lofjord*. Sadly, on the 21st December, 1941, she was badly damaged by a fire in which 28 Germans died. Later, her engines and most of her fittings were removed and the hulk was used by the Luftwaffe as a target for bombing practice. In July, 1943, it was towed by a German tug to Gilléleje in Denmark and beached. When the fire became known to the British press, *Lloyd's List* greeted the news with mixed feelings: 'The loss of *Black Prince* is gratifying in so far as an important ship is denied to Germany but her destruction recalls that she, with her sister ship, was one of the most ingeniously designed vessels ever built for North Sea passenger and mail service...... The pair will go down in history as an example of the almost perfect motorships of their class.'

Surprisingly, after the War *Black Prince (i)*'s hull was found to be in good enough condition for Olsens to consider using it as the basis for a new ship. In the end, however, it was sold to another owner who also had this idea but eventually the scheme was abandoned and the sad remains of this once-fine liner were sold for scrap.

The sister, *Black Watch (i)*, was also taken over by the Germans for use as an accommodation ship for U-Boat crews. For a time she was stationed at Kirkenes, close to the Russian border, and later she lay at Hammerfest. No doubt many of her German submariner 'guests' were among those who harried the Allied convoys, including Norwegian vessels, which ran the gauntlet in order to take supplies to the northern Russian ports in the notorious Arctic convoys. Finally, *Black Watch (i)* was moved to a base in Kilbotn Bay, near Harstad. Strangely, unlike her sister, she kept her English name. She very nearly survived the War but at 4 pm on the 4th May, 1945 – just three days before the German forces in Norway surrendered and four days before the Allies declared Victory in Europe – she was attacked by aircraft from the British carriers H.M.S. *Queen*, H.M.S. *Searcher* and H.M.S. *Trumpeter*. Wracked by explosions and fire, she broke in two and sank. Two other vessels were also destroyed and it was reported that, in all, more than 400 U-Boat officers and crew perished. One of the pilots involved in the attack, Flight Commander Dennis J. Bunyan, later had a strong Norwegian connection as the New York representative of the Bergen Bank. In an account of the attack which was published in the Fred. Olsen house journal *Linjen* in 1983, he wrote: 'I only feel badly that such a good-looking ship had to be sent to the bottom. My regrets to Fred. Olsen..... c'est la guerre!' After the War, the authorities considered blowing up the wreck but it was decided that this would be too dangerous and it was eventually removed by more conventional means.

The *Blenheim (i)* was also taken over by the Germans, who used her as a troopship. However, on the 22nd April, 1941 she caught fire and exploded in Porsangerfjord while carrying a full load of German troops and vehicles. 138 men died. Sabotage was suspected and a number of crew members were arrested but, after they had been interrogated, it was concluded that the disaster had been caused by accident.

Blenheim (i)'s elderly sister, *Bessheim*, did not survive much longer. While approaching Hammerfest on the 21st November, 1941, she was apparently torpedoed and sunk by the British submarine H.M.S. *Seawolf*. As so often on these occasions, however, there is a conflict of evidence – some sources suggest she struck a mine which had been laid by a Russian submarine. If she was, indeed, hit by a torpedo, this was the second time it had happened; but on the earlier occasion, just over two months previously, she had remained afloat.

The *Paris (ii)* was also a war casualty. At the time of the invasion, she was laid up at Fredrikstad but, like the *Bessheim*, *Brabant (iii)* and *Bali*, she was requisitioned by the Germans for transport duties along the coast of northern Norway. Later, they used her as a mother ship for minesweepers. On the 12th March, 1945, however, she was sailing in a convoy off Haugesund when she was sunk by two torpedoes from the British motor torpedo boat M.T.B. *711*. 86 lives were lost. Although much less modern and commodious than *Black Watch (i)*, she too would have been very useful to Olsens if only she could have survived until the War ended a few weeks later.

Survivors.

The Fred. Olsen passenger fleet was therefore reduced to just three ships. The fine, modern *Bretagne (iii)* had been taken by the Kriegsmarine for use as an accommodation ship in early 1941 and had later acted as a troop transport. Olsens regained possession of her in May, 1945. When the Germans invaded Norway, the *Brabant (iii)* was laid up at Horten but they soon took her up as a transport. Some reports have her sailing regularly between Norway and Germany during the latter stages of the War and claim that she was mined in the Skagerak in October, 1944 but remained afloat. She was finally returned to her owners in September, 1945 after repatriating 700 Germans from northern Norway to Travemünde in their devastated homeland. Earlier, in July, Olsens had received back the steamer *Bali* which had been lying at Kiel. She had been requisitioned by the Kriegsmarine in 1940 and, after a period of transport work, had been converted into a minesweeper. She required a great deal of rebuilding before she could re-enter civilian service.

6.

Post-War Rebuilding

The War ended in Europe in May, 1945 and the Allied nations celebrated. The Norwegian government-in-exile sailed into Oslo on the British liner *Andes*, still in her wartime grey paint and still armed. But, once the celebrations had subsided, the Norwegians, like the people of so many other countries, found that their tribulations were not yet over. This was certainly the case in the shipping industry.

Ships were still at risk from mines which had yet to be cleared; everything was in short supply; and shipowners had a desperate need for new vessels. So much of the pre-War fleet had been lost and many of the remaining vessels, when finally returned to their owners, required lengthy restoration after their wartime service. It was not easy to obtain new tonnage. Many shipyards in Continental Europe had been virtually destroyed and, for some years, supplies of steel and most other materials were desperately limited. As a result, governments found it necessary to impose restrictions and controls. Like many other owners, Fred. Olsen & Co. placed orders for new ships in various countries – wherever they could find a yard with a vacant slot in its schedule – but soon an acute shortage of foreign exchange forced the Norwegian government to place restrictions on the amount of tonnage which could be bought abroad.

Nevertheless, in the years 1946 – 50 the Fred. Olsen companies managed to add 25 ships to their fleet. One of these had been laid down for them before the War but had been left uncompleted; four were members of the huge fleet of standard freighters which the Americans had built during the War; two were former German vessels which had been seized by the Allies; and the rest were new ships ordered from several different yards in Norway, Sweden, Britain and Italy. They were all, however, cargo vessels. The passenger services would have to wait for new tonnage.

The company was, though, faced with a backlog of passenger traffic – many people in Norway, Britain, Belgium, the Netherlands and France had been waiting years to renew old relationships and business links. And there is no doubt that the friendship between Britain and Norway had been enormously strengthened by the ordeal of war. (Every year since 1947, for instance, the city of Oslo has sent a Christmas tree as a present to London to be erected in Trafalgar Square.) Even so, there was little immediate possibility of reviving the tourist trade. Britain's virtual bankruptcy meant that for some years British people were allowed to take no more than £25 out of the country when they went abroad. And in the early post-War period, there was little incentive for tourists to come to Britain. (When, in the summer of 1946, Swedish Lloyd began running their new *Saga* on their Gothenburg

The partially repaired hull of the severely war-damaged *Black Prince (i)* lies at the Hansa Dock, Antwerp on the 26th August, 1947. Plans by Olsens, and later by another shipowner, to restore her to service proved to be unfeasible. *(Newall-Dunn collection)*

Initial construction of the first post-War Olsen passenger ships, *Blenheim (ii)* and *Braemar (i)*, took place at Southampton but they were taken to Oslo to receive their engines and to be fitted out. Here, the incomplete *Braemar (i)* leaves Southampton under tow in late 1952. *(Author's collection)*

to London route, many of her Swedish passengers used her as a hotel while she lay in the Port of London, such was the shortage of food onshore.)

As we have seen, only three Fred. Olsen passenger ships had survived the War. True, there were hopes that the remains of *Black Prince (i)* could be salvaged and restored and, indeed, her hull was towed to Fredrikstad in 1946 and then to Antwerp in 1947. A certain amount of work was done on her but, as noted in a previous chapter, it was found that she could never form the basis of a passenger ship again and although another owner did for a time toy with the idea of converting her into a fruit-carrier, she was sold for scrap in 1951.

The first of the surviving Olsen passenger ships to become available was the *Bretagne (iii)*. In pre-War days she had been an Antwerp ship but now, on the 3rd August, 1945, she started a direct Oslo – Newcastle service. The somewhat dated steamship *Bali* was heavily refitted at Fredrikstad and on the 9th February, 1946 she joined the *Bretagne (iii)* on the Newcastle route. She also made a few voyages to Antwerp. Finally, the *Brabant (iii)* restarted regular Antwerp sailings on the 12th July, 1946 after being refitted at the Aker yard in Oslo.

Sensational new ships.

However, in Olsens' own technical department, plans were being drawn up under the supervision of Leif Steineger for two splendid new liners to replace the lost *Black Prince (i)* and *Black Watch (i)*. Remarkably, each ship was to have two builders. Because the Aker yard was so busy, the construction of the hulls and superstructures was sub-contracted to the Woolston yard of John I. Thornycroft & Co., Ltd. at Southampton. Although it did produce some ships for commercial owners (and in 1939 had been preparing to build a new British Royal Yacht when war intervened and caused the project to be abandoned), this yard was mainly known for its naval vessels. With the War now over, it may therefore have had a less full order book than some other shipbuilders. Once Thornycrofts had launched the incomplete liners, they were to be towed to Oslo where Akers would install the engines and proceed with the fitting-out.

In fact, the launch of the second hull, that of the *Braemar (i)*, nearly ended in disaster. The third Fred. Olsen has written a lively account of the occasion:

'The sponsor of the ship, or as I like to say the godmother, was Mrs. Frances Farquharson, then chatelaine of Braemar Castle......... It was a nice day

The modernistic, streamlined *Braemar (i)* (seen here) and her sister *Blenheim (ii)* caused something of a sensation in the early 1950s. Perhaps their most striking feature was the aerodynamically efficient structure which combined the funnel and the mast. *(Newall-Dunn collection)*

Braemar (i) made an introductory visit to London before entering regular service across the North Sea. Here, on the 23rd May, 1953, the bascules of Tower Bridge are raised to allow her to pass through, accompanied by a tug. *(Author 's collection)*

When *Blenheim (ii)*, named in honour of Winston Churchill, was introduced onto the 'Royal Mail Route' between Oslo and the Tyne in 1951, much favourable comment was aroused by the quality of her furnishings and by their very Norwegian style. *(Bruce Peter collection)*

and, if I remember correctly, the platform for all the guests was covered in green cloth and the Farquharson piper played as the chocks were knocked away to lower the ship onto the ways. When the ship was ready, Sir John Thornycroft handed the bottle to the godmother, who smashed it with gusto and all was quiet – except the chug of a small hydraulic piston to start the ship sliding down the ways, but the hydraulic piston slowed down and then stopped. The ship stood still. You could have heard a pin drop. So after a little while I went and urged the piper to start playing again. He absolutely refused, having orders not to play after the bottle was smashed. After a long and painful wait, the ship decided to move. To my horror, one of the wires coming out of the anchor hawse-pipe slipped out and fell to the ground, leaving only one wire on the port side attached to a large pile of anchor chains, obviously only half of what was needed to stop the ship properly when in her right element. The ship headed for a pier in the distance, where we could see people starting to run towards the shore, and she only stopped after digging her stern into the pier. Afterwards, when the ship was checked, it turned out that only a little bit of paint on the rudder was lacking as the outer part of the pier was made of wood. She had missed the concrete part by only a few yards.

'At the very nice luncheon afterwards, Sir John Thornycroft made a speech to the shipping company and, of course, ended by praising the sponsor who was now anticipating what she would be given for her troubles. But I can assure you that her face fell quite a bit when she was presented with a silver mug.

'The next speech was made by C.N.R. Aamundsen, Managing Director of Akers mek. Verksted in Oslo, who ended by presenting Mrs. Farquharson a bracelet with the name of the ship and Olsen flags in diamonds and sapphires. So all ended well.'

The first of the new ships started her maiden crossing from Oslo to Newcastle on the 30th March, 1951. She was called *Blenheim (ii)* in honour of the great British wartime leader Winston Churchill, who had been born at Blenheim Palace, the Churchill family seat. A large signed photograph of him was hung in the first class observation lounge. The second ship, which followed two years later, was, as we have seen, given the name *Braemar (i)*. This was an oblique tribute to the British Royal family – the village of Braemar, home of the famous Braemar Games, is close to Balmoral, the Monarch's Highland residence. (Over sixty-four years later, a Fred. Olsen passenger ship has actually been called *Balmoral*.)

Although at 4,766 and 4,776 gross tons the new ships were relatively small, they were among the most striking-looking liners of their day. Their fine-lined hulls, whose long, raked bows were decorated with beautiful artworks by Ørnulf Bast and Per Hurum, had a pleasing sheer and were topped by a streamlined superstructure. In particular, there was a solarium on the top deck – a rounded, dome-like structure glazed with plexiglass and open at the rear, which must have been very popular in those sun-loving days. Above everything was a combined signal mast and funnel whose streamlined shape was almost unique and added to the modernistic impression which the ships created. The design of this structure was

the result of a series of wind-tunnel tests and it was notably efficient in throwing the smoke and smuts from the engine well clear of the after decks in almost any weather. With the hull painted in the now-traditional Fred. Olsen grey and topped by a deep white strake and with that shapely funnel carrying the company's buff-yellow livery, each ship was a picture of modern elegance. To reduce top-weight, much of the superstructure was built of aluminium alloy, as were the lifeboats, funnel and masts.

The interiors of these ships were as notable as their exteriors. Once again, the Olsens had commissioned Arnstein Arneberg to design them and again he produced a cleanly modern set of public rooms, strikingly decorated with artworks by Norwegian craftsmen. After visiting the *Braemar (i)*, C. M. Squarey of the travel firm Thos. Cook wrote in the newsletter which he sent to his firm's clients: 'I rate her first-class quarters as nothing short of enchanting'. And a journalist from the trade magazine *The Motor Ship* wrote that 'very few passenger ships of her size are equipped and decorated so artistically and attractively'. An interesting feature on both ships was a large, stylised map of the North Sea. The ship's progress was recorded by a lengthening line of green light which gradually spread along a narrow glass tube linking Oslo and Newcastle. To-day, one of these maps can be seen in the museum at Hvitsten.

The *Blenheim (ii)* could accommodate up to 101 first class passengers, mainly in single cabins but often with inter-connecting doors, 100 in tourist class double-berth cabins and 36 in 'group class' dormitories. There was slightly more emphasis on tourist class in the later *Braemar (i)*. Although quite small, as was acceptable on a ship on such a relatively short route, the first class cabins were notably well fitted-out. A few of them had full private facilities but in the early 1950s it was not thought remarkable that, while most had wash basins with hot and cold running water, it was still necessary for many passengers to don their slippers and dressing gowns and trek down the passage way if they required anything more. As on the pre-War *Black Prince (i)* and *Black Watch (i)*, first class passengers had the use of a Finnish vapour bath.

There were three cargo holds, two of which were refrigerated and were often filled with boxes of fish; and forty cars, lifted on and off by crane, could be carried in a 'tween deck. Later in the ships' lives, this proved to be rather a handicap as the motor tourist trade between Britain and Norway developed to such an extent that a much larger capacity for cars was required.

In 1953, the same year that Olsens introduced the *Braemar (i)*, the rival Bergen Line brought out their new *Leda*. Inevitably, comparisons were made, especially when the *Leda* made a promotional visit to Oslo (during which, embarrassingly, she ran aground with King Haakon on board). The Bergen ship scored over her rivals from Oslo by being fitted with Denny-Brown fin-type stabilisers which, although developed in the 1930s, were only now beginning to come into widespread use. There is no doubt that on the often stormy North Sea this gave her an advantage. On the other hand, the passenger quarters on the Olsen twins were fully air-conditioned throughout and her first class rooms were, to some tastes, more handsomely furnished. With the Swedish Lloyd also introducing new ships, these were exciting times on the North Sea.

When the *Blenheim (ii)* entered service on the Oslo – Newcastle route, she was able to reinstate the intermediate call at Kristiansand. At first, her partner in a twice-weekly schedule was the slightly slower *Bretagne (iii)* which omitted that call. The *Bali* was now free to join *Brabant (iii)* in the Oslo – Antwerp service, which could thus be maintained on a weekly basis. Although brochures still advertised train connections between Antwerp and Paris, there was less emphasis on passenger traffic on this route than there had been in pre-War days and *Brabant (iii)* was carrying a maximum of 80 passengers in first, second and group classes, while *Bali*'s passenger capacity had been reduced to just 40.

Braemar (i) entered service in May, 1953 and joined her sister on the Newcastle run. *Bretagne (iii)* was now transferred to the Antwerp route, whereupon *Bali*, which had finally been converted to oil-firing in 1950, was sold to the Burmese Shipping Board who used her for coastal service. Passenger service on the Oslo – Antwerp route did not last much longer, however. The *Brabant (iii)* was sold to Sudanese owners at the end of 1954 and the *Bretagne (iii)* went to the Hellenic Mediterranean Line of Piraeus in 1958. Thereafter, although Fred. Olsen continued sailings to Antwerp and Rotterdam and other Continental ports using a fleet of specially-designed and extremely versatile freighters which could accommodate a wide variety of different cargoes, passenger-carrying ceased on these routes.

A change of guard.

Unfortunately, Consul General Rudolf Olsen had not lived to enjoy the triumph of the *Blenheim (ii)*'s introduction. He died on the 14th February, 1951, six weeks before her first sailing. He had been the more outgoing, the more public of the two brothers. Only four years later, a further crisis hit the firm. Thomas, the surviving brother, suffered a stroke and, although he lived on until 1969, he was never able to resume an active rôle in the business. Thus, in 1955, at the age of twenty-six, the third Fred. Olsen suddenly found himself assuming the daunting task of managing and developing the family empire

A more recent photograph of the third Fred. Olsen who, at the age of 26, had been forced to take on the responsibilities of running the widespread family business when his father, Thomas Olsen, became ill in 1955. *(Fred. Olsen & Co.)*

7.
Sailing to the Sun

As we have seen in an earlier chapter, the Olsens had begun running ships to and from the Spanish-owned Canary Islands in the early 1920s. Things had not always been easy for them on this route, with exports of bananas to Britain being affected by the policy of Imperial Preference, which favoured trade with countries within the Empire, including the banana-exporting islands of the British West Indies. To make matters worse, during the years of the left-wing Republican government and then during the Civil War, much of the Canaries' produce was diverted to mainland Spain. Then, the Civil War had been quickly followed by the Second World War. Nevertheless, the routes from the Canary Islands to London and, for a time, to Liverpool had soon regained their importance for the Fred. Olsen Line. It was not until the mid-1960s, however, that Olsens started full-scale passenger service to the islands.

They had, of course, been well-established in the North Sea passenger business for many years. In addition, they had offered comfortable cabin accommodation for a handful of passengers on their freighters on most of their other routes, including those to South America and the American West Coast. But, even so, they had never been major competitors in the deep-sea passenger business. This was, perhaps, fortunate since by the mid-1950s aeroplanes were poaching many of the travellers who previously had little alternative but to go by ship. This trend accelerated with the coming of the jet airliners, at first on the North Atlantic from 1958 onwards and later on the other oceans.

By the mid-1960s, the outlook for long-distance passenger shipping seemed very bleak indeed. Some companies tried to find employment for a few of their redundant passenger ships by switching them to cruising. Sometimes they were successful, as with Union-Castle's heavily converted *Reina del Mar*, but such large, class-divided and enclosed liners as the famous *Queen Mary* proved unsuited to this new rôle. However, trends were beginning to appear in the travel and tourism industries which offered hope for those shipowners who had the courage to risk large sums of money in building vessels specifically for a new type of cruising.

To borrow a famous phrase from Harold Macmillan, many people had 'never had it so good' – they were better off than ever before. And because of the advent of cheap charter flights, travel companies could now offer holidays abroad to people who could never previously have considered them. Perhaps some of these new travellers could be persuaded to take a cruise. Most of the shipowners who dared to take up this challenge were Norwegians – in some cases speculating with profits they had made in the tanker market. New lines such as Royal Caribbean, Norwegian Caribbean and Royal Viking were formed by well-known owners in Oslo and Bergen with the intention of concentrating almost entirely on the American market. Olsens, on the other hand, turned to the British market since, with their North Sea routes, they were already established there.

A further factor which precipitated Olsens' entry into cruising was the development of motor tourism. The Olsen passenger ships had always carried numbers of tourists to Norway in the summer months and for some years provision had been made for these travellers to take their cars with them, if they so wished. As we have seen, the *Blenheim (ii)* and the *Braemar (i)* of 1951 and 1953 each had 'tween decks with space for about forty cars, which were lifted on and off by crane. Now, however, with the growth of car ownership and motor travel generally, other lines on other routes were introducing more sophisticated vehicle-carrying

A sunlit scene at Santa Cruz de Tenerife in the early 1920s with the *San Andres* still wearing Thoresen funnel colours. Note her array of ventilators intended to keep her perishable cargoes cool. A coaster lies alongside her. (*Postcard, Newall-Dunn collection*)

passenger ships onto which much larger numbers of cars could be driven through doors, either in the side of the hull or at the bow or the stern. The *Blenheim (ii)* and *Braemar (i)* did not have this facility and, although they were beautiful ships and still relatively young, they were already out of date and, by the mid-1960s, unable to cope with the increasing demand for car spaces in the summer months.

Innovative sisters.

Olsens were not alone in encountering this problem. Their long-time competitors for the passenger traffic between Britain and Norway, the Bergen Line (Det Bergenske Dampskibsselskab), were also experiencing demand for more car spaces than their famous *Venus* and *Leda* could offer. The third Fred. Olsen discussed the problem with Erik Waaler, the managing director of the Bergen company and, as a result, the rival owners co-operated to develop two of the most remarkable and successful multi-purpose ships which have ever been built.

Fred. Olsen's deputy technical director, John Johnsen, and his department produced a design for a vessel of 9,500 gross tons which in the summer months could carry 587 passengers across the North Sea in two classes and could also take up to 184 cars, loaded over a ramp at the stern. Out of season, the ship would be switched to Olsen's Canary Islands service, for which the lower car decks could be converted into refrigerated space for the carriage of tomatoes and other produce. For some years, John Johnsen and his team had, with the close involvement of the third Fred. Olsen, been devising efficient new methods of cargo-handling, often with freight being assembled on pallets and then loaded and unloaded through 'ports' (i.e.: apertures) in the sides of the ship. Now, for the new vessel, they designed a system of conveyors, elevators and specially-built electric fork-lift trucks which could load and stow an entire palletised cargo in as little as six hours. The highly-mechanised system on board was to be matched by equally ingenious equipment in specially-built warehouses which would receive the Canary Islands produce when the ship arrived at Millwall Dock in the Port of London.

The third Fred. Olsen had commissioned a young architect called Norman Foster, who of course later became world-famous, to

Progress comes to cargo-handling: a fork-lift truck unloads palletised cargo from a Fred. Olsen freighter in 1965. Olsens were notable pioneers of new systems which markedly improved efficiency and reduced the time ships needed to spend in port. *(Newall-Dunn collection)*

The complex of passenger terminal, cargo sheds and workers' social facilities built at Millwall Dock in the Port of London for Fred. Olsen's Canary Islands service in the mid-1960s was a very important early commission for the young architect Norman Foster. *(Foster & Partners)*

The combined fruit-carrier / cruise ship / car ferry launched at Lübeck in March, 1965 was a joint venture between Olsens, for whom she sailed as *Black Watch (ii)*, and the Bergen Line who called her *Jupiter*. For the occasion, both names were painted on her bow and forefoot. *(Newall-Dunn collection)*

design a passenger terminal in the same complex at Millwall, and also a modern, glass-walled social centre where employees could eat and relax. Foster has freely acknowledged that this commission was a crucial turning point in his career. Until then, he had been so short of work that he had considered emigrating but now the Fred. Olsen buildings brought him to the attention of several other important clients. Olsen and Foster had similar views on the importance of architecture as a social influence and in later years Foster received further commissions from Olsen – a survey to determine how the island of La Gomera in the Canaries could be developed without damaging its coastline or destroying its social fabric (see Chapter Nine); modernisation of the Fred. Olsen passenger office in Regent Street, London (again

A picture of one of *Black Watch (ii)*'s two high-speed Pielstick V18-cylinder main engines while it was still at the Ottensener Eisenwerke engine-building facility at Hamburg prior to being installed in the ship. *(Newall-Dunn collection)*

with full-height glass walls); and plans for a new head office near Hvitsten. This last project was never built since the deterioration in the climate in the shipping industry in the mid-1970s persuaded Olsen that it should be dropped.

Reverting to the new ship, it was not only her cargo facilities which were notable. Her passenger spaces would not be wasted in the winter months. When on the Canaries cargo run, she could also act as a passenger liner and Olsens would be able to offer the round trip as a voyage to the sun. The idea of carrying passengers on 'fruiters' sailing to and from the Canary Islands was not new. The Liverpool-based produce importers Yeoward Bros. had very successfully offered this facility on their vessels from the early 1900s until they withdrew from shipowning in 1954 and the Aznar Line of Bilbao had later revived the service, again from Liverpool.

When the new Fred. Olsen / Bergen Line ship was running to the Canaries, the smaller ferry cabins would be closed off but the larger ones, all with toilets and either a bath or a shower, would remain in use and there would be comfortable accommodation for 350 one-class passengers. Olsens were, in fact, entering the cruise market. The ease with which the ship could be converted from a high-density ferry into a comfortable cruise ship was remarkable. For instance, the busy ferry cafeteria could be transformed into an elegant restaurant simply by shuttering off the food service counters at one end of the room. Even more ingeniously, the indoor lido with sunken swimming pool and retractable glass-panelled roof, which was a feature of the ship when she was cruising, could be transformed into a lounge when she was in ferry mode. The swimming pool would be decked over and seating would be installed for passengers who had not booked cabins. The now enclosed void which had been the swimming pool became a store room for the duty free shop! As Bruce Peter observes, 'Not an inch of space was wasted on this ship'. Amazingly, the entire conversion from ferry to cruise ship, or vice versa, could be completed in perhaps 50 hours.

The new ship was flexible in another way. She had two owners and two registered names. In the Summer, she ran on the Bergen Line's Newcastle – Bergen route under their traditional name of *Jupiter* but when employed in Fred. Olsen's Canary Islands service in the winter months, she was called *Black Watch (ii)*, thus reviving the name of the mini-liner which had made such an impression during her

When sailing on winter voyages to the Canaries, passengers on both *Black Watch (ii)* and *Black Prince (ii)* could enjoy this indoor pool and its surrounding lido area. In good weather, the retractable roof overhead could, as seen here, be slid open. *(Postcard, John Sutherland collection)*

When the sisters were serving as North Sea ferries, the swimming pool was covered in and the lido area was transformed into a comfortable lounge. It was typical of the ingenuity of the ships' design that the now enclosed pool became a storage space for the duty free shop. *(Bruce Peter collection)*

The first of the two sisters makes her maiden arrival on the Tyne as the Bergen Line's *Jupiter* on the 2nd July, 1966. Her funnel bears the Bergen company's flag which would be replaced by that of Fred. Olsen whenever she sailed as *Black Watch (ii)*. (*Author's collection*)

brief life before the War. Ownership was divided, 52% by Olsens and 48% by the Bergen company. During each seasonal conversion, the ship's name would be changed on both bow and stern and a reproduction of the appropriate company flag would be attached to each side of her funnel.

A sister ship, ordered slightly later, was at first entirely owned by the Fred. Olsen company A/S Ganger Rolf and was called *Black Prince (ii)*. In the Summer, she too ran across the North Sea but on a new route, different from Olsens' traditional Oslo – Newcastle run. Her Norwegian terminal was at Kristiansand and from there she operated what became known as the 'pendulum service', alternating round trips to Amsterdam and to Harwich. Out of season, she joined her sister on the Canary Islands run.

The two sisters were claimed to be the largest car ferries then in existence and had a very distinctive appearance which made them instantly recognisable. In addition to the bold artworks on their stems, they had unusual bow window-shaped bridge-fronts and aerodynamic funnels which, to some eyes, were reminiscent of Viking helmets. Apart from having different bow decorations, the two ships were virtually identical, both externally and internally, and when they happened to be in port together it was not unknown for passengers to return unwittingly to the wrong ship.

In the mid-1960s, German yards were eager to re-enter the passenger shipbuilding business and the contracts for the new vessels were won by the Lübecker Flender Werke of Lübeck, who undoubtedly produced two extremely sturdy vessels. The hulls were strengthened for navigation through ice and were given efficient bulbous bows, fin stabilisers, side-thrusters and controllable-pitch propellers. Each ship was driven by two V18-cylinder Pielstick diesel engines. Passenger spaces were entirely air-conditioned.

At the time of her introduction, her proud owners described *Black Watch (ii)* / *Jupiter* as 'the most complete passenger/cargo vessel in the World'.

Instant popularity.

The *Black Watch (ii)* / *Jupiter* entered Bergen Line service in the early summer of 1966 and then made her first voyage from London to the Canaries for Fred. Olsen in the September. The following month, Olsens took delivery of *Black Prince (ii)* which thereupon joined her sister on the Canary Islands route. Although the passage across the Bay of Biscay could sometimes be rough, the new weekly Canary Islands passenger service proved to be an enormous success and *Black Watch (ii)* and *Black Prince (ii)* became extremely popular with a public who appreciated a reasonably-priced, civilised cruise to the sun. Each 13-day round trip started on Thursday afternoon from London, Millwall Dock and called at Arecife (on the island of Lanzarote), Las Palmas de Gran Canaria, Santa Cruz de Tenerife and again at Las Palmas de Gran Canaria. It now seems incredible that prices ranged from just £69 to £150. It was also possible to book a one-way voyage in either direction for £35 upwards.

In the 1960s, there was a great deal of strife in the Port of London and Olsens' introduction of their new cargo-handling systems prompted what the company considered to be excessive demands from the dockers' union. As a result of the disagreement which followed, the dockers went on strike in January, 1967 and *Black Watch (ii)* sailed from Millwall Dock with passengers but without cargo. The company threatened to suspend the service altogether but in the end the situation was resolved.

Beauty in a hurry: an aerial view of *Black Watch (ii)* at speed, displaying her unusual streamlined funnel, her fine-lined hull and her ferry stem with its ramp door which could be lowered to give access to the vehicle deck. *(Newall-Dunn collection)*

On a couple of occasions during that first 1966-67 season, a call was also made at Funchal on the beautiful island of Madeira and this proved to be so popular with passengers that from then onwards almost all voyages included this call. Every winter since 1948, the Bergen Line's famous old *Venus* had been making winter voyages to Madeira either from Plymouth or Southampton but she was nearing the end of her career and was withdrawn in 1968, leaving the Madeira run to Olsens. *Black Prince (ii)*, although no longer operating a regular service to the island, continues to this day to be a frequent visitor and by April, 1999 was making her 500th call at Funchal.

In his book *Passenger Liners Scandinavian Style*, Bruce Peter describes his first encounter with one of the sisters, when she was sailing as the Bergen Line's *Jupiter*:

'As we drove along the quayside to board, it was possible to make out the painted-out silhouette letters of her alter ego *Black Watch* welded into the *Jupiter*'s hull. It suddenly dawned on me that this was the same ship about which my great-aunt had enthused. A lover of cruising, she favoured the *Black*

Watch over all others, liking her small scale, congenial staff and her cleanliness. We drove aboard and a group of seamen manhandled the car down a hatch into a cargo hold below the main car deck. We then climbed up to the main foyer, which was carpeted in

An advertisement in the travel press in November, 1965 announces the start of Olsen's passenger service to the Canaries the following year. The artist's impression of the new ships is perhaps a little fanciful. *(Newall-Dunn collection)*

The new *Black Prince (ii)* lies at the Millwall Dock terminal in the Port of London on the 19th October, 1966, preparing for her maiden voyage to the Canaries. Note the open cargo doors in the ship's side and, again, the retractable glazed roof over the indoor lido. *(Newall-Dunn collection)*

Black Watch tartan – another reminder of the *Jupiter*'s other rôle. Despite this dubious *(sic)* choice, the space was very elegant...... with carved woodwork and decorative brass balustrades on the two curving staircases, between which hung a fine portrait of King Olav and Queen Martha of Norway. The interiors left one in no doubt that this was a proud Norwegian ship and, although space seemed confined in places, little expense had been spared in furnishing it to the highest standards.'

Bruce Peter was particularly impressed by the Westminster Lounge, which he describes as:

'a beautiful circular room with a centrally-located dance floor and vertically slatted screens to make quiet corners. The combination of wood panelling, indirect lighting and dark green upholstery made a warm and cosy atmosphere.'

The equivalent lounge is still charming passengers on *Black Prince (ii)* to-day.

Harwich had no doubt been chosen as the British terminal for Olsen's summertime North Sea ferry service because it was conveniently situated to tap the tourist traffic to and from the South of England. Meanwhile, however, the *Blenheim (ii)* and *Braemar (i)* continued to run their habitual service between Oslo, Kristiansand and the northern port of Newcastle.

Unfortunately, on the 21st May, 1968, *Blenheim (ii)* met disaster when a fire broke out in her first class dining room. It quickly took hold and, while some officers and crew members remained on board in an attempt to control the blaze, the passengers and the rest of the crew were ordered to take to the lifeboats. They were picked up by Danish fishing boats and by Dutch and Danish helicopters, many being transferred to the *Braemar (i)* which had rushed to the aid of her stricken sister. In the true spirit of the sea, the rival Ellerman's Wilson Line's *Spero* also stood by in case further help were needed. Fortunately, no lives were lost. Eventually, the blaze was extinguished by two salvage tugs and the ravaged ship was towed to Kristiansand. *Blenheim (ii)*'s captain, who had remained on his ship, had to be rushed to hospital suffering from exhaustion. The superstructure and passenger accommodation had been almost completely destroyed but the hull, engines and much of the cargo (including 50 new cars) were largely undamaged. The remains of this once-beautiful vessel were eventually sold to other Norwegian owners, who had her converted into a specialist car-carrier. The *Braemar (i)* now maintained the Oslo – Kristiansand – Newcastle service on her own until she was withdrawn in 1975. By then, she was the last old-style liner still in service on the North Sea. She had been an extremely popular ship and many people gathered to bid her farewell as she sailed from the Tyne for the last time.

By 1975 *Braemar (i)*, although still only twenty-two years old, had become the last orthodox passenger / cargo ferry sailing on the North Sea. After her retirement she was sold to become *The Philippine Tourist*, a casino ship, seen here in a faint but very rare photograph taken at Manila. *(Ambrose Greenway collection)*

A larger running mate.

Meanwhile, the success of *Black Watch (ii)* and *Black Prince (ii)* had prompted Olsens to order a similar but larger ship. The contract to build the *Blenheim (iii)* was won, with the help of a financial contribution from the British government, by the famous Clydebank yard of John Brown & Co., Ltd., which was now part of Upper Clyde Shipbuilders. Browns were desperate for work which would keep their fitting-out department occupied once they had completed the *Queen Elizabeth 2* and in order to gain the contract they quoted a very keen price of £4 million and guaranteed delivery by the 21st February, 1970. Trade union officials gave a pledge of 'full co-operation' but, unhappily, labour troubles, persistent theft and other difficulties hampered progress and, far from being able to deliver the ship on time, the yard could not

even launch her until the 10th January. Although the third Fred. Olsen made complimentary remarks about the standard of workmanship, the occasion cannot have been a cordial one. The terms of the contract meant that the shipyard had to pay Olsens compensation for late delivery and the 10,420 gross tons *Blenheim (iii)* became the fourth passenger ship in succession on which Brown's had lost money. Upper Clyde Shipbuilders decreed that no more passenger ships would be built at a yard which, in its time, had been responsible for such great liners as the *Lusitania*, *Aquitania*, *Queen Mary*, *Queen Elizabeth* and *Queen Elizabeth 2*.

The delay was extremely inconvenient for Olsens. The *Blenheim (iii)* had been due to take over the Kristiansand – Harwich service and they not only had to charter a smaller vessel called the *Vikingfjord* to deputise for her but

The late delivery of *Blenheim (iii)* in 1970 meant that the Fred. Olsen Line had to charter the *Vikingfjord*, which was German-owned despite her Norwegian name. In this photograph, she is wearing Olsen funnel colours. *(Newall-Dunn collection)*

The new *Blenheim (iii)*, an enlarged version of the very successful *Black Watch (ii)* and *Black Prince (ii)*, finally ran her trials on the Clyde in September, 1970. In the background is a small CaledonianMacBrayne ferry. *(Author's collection)*

Passengers crowd the rails on the starboard side as *Blenheim (iii)* pulls briskly away from the quayside, shewing off her ferry stern. With motor tourism growing rapidly, she had been designed to carry many more vehicles than her smaller running-mates.
(Newall-Dunn collection)

This picture of *Blenheim (iii)*'s enclosed swimming pool and lido clearly shews the glass-panelled roof which could be slid open in fine weather — a feature not only on the Olsen ships but also on several other well-known liners of the late 1960s and early 1970s. *(Fred. Olsen & Co.)*

they also had to send some passengers by air. However, the new ship was finally delivered in September, 1970 and entered the wintertime London – Canaries service. She started her first Kristiansand – Harwich season in May, 1971. In later years, she also appeared on the Newcastle route. Under the terms of the government building subsidy, she flew the British flag and was manned by a British crew.

About twenty feet longer than *Black Watch (ii)* and *Black Prince (ii)*, she could carry 995 passengers, all in one class, when in ferry mode and 300 cars (as against 184 on the older ships – so much had motor traffic expanded in four years). She too was a very pleasantly furnished ship, slightly more modern in style than her running-mates. Like them, she had interiors designed by the Norwegian architects Barstad & Skjæveland with the third Fred. Olsen and his wife Kristin 'taking a very close interest'. Her two V8-cylinder Pielstick engines had been built by Crossley-Premier. Unfortunately, like many vessels which have had a difficult birth, she proved to be rather troublesome – she sometimes found it hard to maintain her scheduled speed

and had several engine breakdowns. Nevertheless, she was popular with many of her passengers and had many good qualities. Years later, when she had long since passed out of the Olsen fleet, Captain Roland Parent, then a pilot in the port of Fort Lauderdale, handled her regularly. He later told the author that she was one of his favourite ships and, in a trade which perhaps made fewer demands on her, she was almost completely reliable.

In 1968, Olsens had sold a part-interest in *Black Prince (ii)* to the Bergen Line on terms roughly similar to those which applied to *Black Watch (ii)* / *Jupiter* except that in this case ownership was divided 60% by Fred. Olsen and 40% by Bergen. From 1970 onwards she ran in the summer months as the *Venus* in conjunction with her sister on the Bergen company's North Sea routes, while still operating for Olsens as *Black Prince (ii)* in the wintertime. However, in anticipation of the expected arrival of the *Blenheim (iii)* on the London – Madeira – Canaries route, they now used her to start a new fortnightly winter service from Rotterdam to Madeira and the Canaries, catering for Dutch and German passengers

The forward-facing Saga Lounge, a comfortable space much liked by *Blenheim (iii)*'s mainly British passengers. Her public rooms were particularly well-furnished, but in a slightly more modern style than those on her running-mates. *(Fred.Olsen & Co.)*

The Viking Lounge on *Blenheim (iii)*. Cruise ships in the 1970s provided their passengers with rather less organised entertainment than the vessels of to-day but then, as now, ballroom dancing was very popular. *(Bruce Peter collection)*

8.
Ferry Developments

Fred. Olsen & Co. first became involved in the new-style ferry trades carrying large numbers of motor vehicles as well as passengers in 1961, when they became the agents and also part-owners of a new service being established between Oslo and the German port of Kiel by another major Norwegian shipowner, Anders Jahre, under the name Jahre Line. Then in October, 1968, Olsens bought a stake in a very modem car ferry which had been running unprofitably between Copenhagen and the Norwegian ports of Brevik and Fredrikstad. The 3,612-ton *Kobenhavn* had been completed two years previously by the Orenstein-Koppel & Lübecker Maschinenbau company of Lübeck in Germany for the Oslo shipowners Sverre Ditlev-Simonsen & Co. They operated her under the trade name Den Norske Kobenhavenlinje (the Norwegian Copenhagen Line). Small though she was by the standards of the day, she was an important vessel, an early member of a long and gradually evolving series of ferries — and eventually cruise ships — designed by Tage Wandborg of the Copenhagen naval architects Knud E. Hansen A/S. Wandborg was hugely influential in establishing the shape of a whole generation of modem passenger ships and the *Kobenhavn* was a typical example of his early work, sleek and modernistic and with a panoramic sun lounge on the top deck. Olsens now acquired a 60% interest in her and, under their own colours, began running her between Oslo and Copenhagen via Brevik and Horten and also between Brevik, Gothenburg and Copenhagen. On the Oslo — Copenhagen run, however, she was in competition with the Danish ships of the DFDS company, who were well established with a direct service between the two capital cities, and in less than a year the *Kobenhavn* was withdrawn. She was chartered out, at first to a French shipping company and then to the Larvik-Fredrikshavn Line. Eventually, she was sold to Chilean owners.

Kristiansand the hub.

More successful was Olsens' outright purchase in September, 1968 of the A/S Kristiansands Dampskipsselskap (Kristiansand Steamship Company, often known simply as KDS). Together with the introduction of *Black Prince (ii)*'s 'pendulum' services to Harwich and to Amsterdam in 1967, this established Kristiansand as the centre for Fred. Olsen's new involvement in the car ferry trades.

KDS dated back to 1899 and was one of the many small shipping companies which had been set up in ports

The purchase of a majority stake in the sleek little *Kobenhavn* in 1968 was part of Fred. Olsen's move into the growing ferry trade between Norway and Denmark. She was unsuccessful, however, and was eventually sold. *(Newall-Dunn collection)*

The acquisition of the KDS company with its Skagerak Express service was much happier. One of the vessels included in the purchase was the small *Skagen*, seen here in a later incarnation as the *Borgholm*, a depot ship for mini-submarines. *(Bruce Peter collection)*

around the Norwegian coast in order to serve local needs. Its main interest was in providing a link across the Skagerak to Hirtshals in Denmark. This was a 4-hour crossing, much shorter than those on the *København*'s lengthier route. When bought by Olsens, KDS had two yellow-hulled ferries, the 1,831-ton *Skagen* and the newly-built 2.681-ton *Christian IV* (aptly named after the king who had ruled both Denmark and Norway at the turn of the sixteenth and seventeenth centuries). These two vessels carried not only foot-passengers and motor vehicles but also railway wagons. For that reason, railway lines were sunk into the surface of the car decks. The *Skagen* went on to have an unusual after-life, being transferred to Fred. Olsen Oceanics as the *Borgholm (iv)* in 1975 and converted into a depot ship for mini-submarines. For many years, one of the KDS company's idiosyncrasies had been that, owing to the strong principles of its then owners, it did not serve alcohol on its ships. This was, to say the least, unusual on ferries operating on international routes and with a change of ownership came a change of policy.

In 1971, the Skagerak Express, as the Kristiansand — Hirtshals service had become known, was boosted by the introduction of another of the Fred. Olsen technical department's ingeniously designed multi-purpose vessels — albeit a smaller and rather less glamorous one than the cruise-ferries *Black Watch (ii)*, *Black Prince (ii)* and *Blenheim (iii)*. The 2,714-ton *Buenavista (ii)* was built by the Ulstein Mekaniske Verksted of Ulsteinvik, and, while still able to carry railway wagons, was mainly intended to cope with the growing car traffic on the route in the summer months and also to increase the line's capacity to carry lorries and trailers. Out of season, she was intended for freight-only voyages between the Canaries and European ports, carrying tomatoes and vegetables in refrigerated holds and also miscellaneous cargo on pallets. A remarkable feature of her design was that when, every year, she was converted for this winter employment, her interior passenger quarters, which were fully air-conditioned, could be completely removed to make more

space for cargo. At the same time, six of her eight lifeboats would be removed, In one small respect, she resembled the *Black Watch (ii)*, *Black Prince (ii)* and *Blenheim (iii)* — her bridge had a 'bow window' front.

The following year, the Ulstein yard delivered a near-sister ship, the *Bonanza (ii)*. In addition to service on the Skagerak route, both vessels spent quite long periods on charter to other ferry operators — during the first few months of her career, for instance, the *Bonanza (iv)* ran between Finland and Sweden for the Silja Line. In 1974, the *Buenavista (ii)* was lengthened by the insertion of a new mid-section, which increased her gross tonnage to 3,282 and gave her a long, low and rather graceful look. She could now carry up to 900 deck passengers and 160 cars. In 1977, she was sold to Amsterdamse Maritiem Transport Maatschapij BV, a Dutch company associated with Fred. Olsen. Meanwhile, the *Bonanza (ii)* continued to run for KDS until 1980. Both of these remarkable ships will crop up again in Chapter Nine, when we deal with the ferry services around the Canary Islands and to Morocco.

Another cruise-ferry.

A further addition to Olsens' growing ferry fleet came in 1973 when the Dubigeon-Normandie shipyard at Nantes on the River Loire delivered the 11,344-ton *Bolero*. She too was a versatile vessel since she was equally suitable either for service as a car ferry or as a comfortable cruise ship. Unlike her companions in the Olsen passenger fleet, however, she had not been specifically designed to meet the company's requirements. In fact, she was to some extent a 'standard product', similar in design and appearance to a whole series of substantial-looking 11,000- and 12,000-tonners which the Dubigeon company built for various owners. Powered by French-built Pielstick high speed diesels, these vessels were instantly recognisable, with their flat but raked superstructure fronts and their large twin side-by-side funnels.

The *Bolero* was initially owned by a consortium of well-known Norwegian owners, which included not only

Olsens but also Fearnley & Eger, J. Ludwig Mowinckels and Roald P. Aukner, and had been ordered for a proposed ferry service between Travemünde in Germany and the Swedish port of Södertiilje, ten miles from Stockholm. In the event, the project was abandoned and other employment had to be found for her. After several voyages between Hamburg and Harwich under charter to the Prinzen Line, she crossed the Atlantic with her car deck laden with German automobiles which were being exported to the United States. Having arrived in America, she ran for the next three summer seasons as a joint venture with Lion Ferries of Sweden in a ferry service between Portland (Maine) and Yarmouth (Nova Scotia). Each winter the *Bolero* would sail for Miami, from where she ran for Commodore Cruise Line, a company founded by a hotel and travel trade entrepreneur called Sanford Chobol who used chartered ships for Caribbean cruises, and now became a joint venture with the Swedish company Wallenius.

In 1975, Fred. Olsen took delivery of yet another multi-purpose vessel. In a fleet notable for the good looks of its passenger ships, the *Borgen (ii)* had an uncharacteristically chunky appearance. As on many ferries at that time, the exhaust from her engines was led upwards through pipes at either side of the car deck in order to leave as much uninterrupted space as possible. As a result, she had twin side-by-side funnels. A product of the Aalborg yard in Denmark, she was driven by four 6-cylinder Stork-Werkspoor diesel engines, which were quite powerful for a 5,330ton vessel. As with so many post-War Olsen ships, her designers had paid particular attention to speedy loading and unloading and the *Borgen (ii)* not only had both a bow ramp and a stem ramp but also side doors. Her hull was strengthened for navigation through ice and she was designed to be particularly manoeuvrable.

Since she was mainly intended for the Kristiansand — Hirtshals ferry route, her car deck was, as usual, equipped with rail tracks. For the same reason, most of her 776 passengers travelled in reclining seats or were expected to linger in the restaurant, the cafeteria or the panoramic bar. She did, though, have double and four-berth cabins for 254 and could therefore be used on longer routes if required. Indeed, after a few weeks on the Hirtshals run, she singlehandedly maintained the new joint Fred. Olsen / Bergen Line service on the Newcastle — Norway routes (see below) throughout the autumn and winter of 1975-6. She then had a season on the Kristiansand — Harwich run but afterwards was mainly confined to the Skagerak

OPPOSITE: The faithful *Christian IV*, pictured at Kristiansand, was one of the stalwarts of the KDS service until the traffic outgrew her. She and the other ships not only carried passengers and motor vehicles but also railway wagons.
(Bruce Peter collection)

Buenavista after being lengthened. She was one of two extraordinarily adaptable vessels designed to meet the very differing requirements of the short Skagerak Express ferry crossing and the Canary Islands fruit trade. Here she is seen while under charter to the Viking Line. *(Bruce Peter collection)*

Express service, for which, in truth, she was better suited. Traffic on the route was increasing to such an extent that in 1981 she was sent back to her builders for a drastic reconstruction. She was cut in two amidships and a new 20 metre-long section was inserted; more unusually, she was also split horizontally so that an extra car deck could be put in place. When, in 1982, she emerged from this complicated rebuilding, she had a gross tonnage of 7,570, could carry up to 1,622 passengers and a maximum of 430 cars but whatever good looks she had once had were now utterly lost.

It is interesting to note that it was with KDS that a member of a fifth generation of Olsens assumed

responsibility within the group when the third Fred. Olsen's daughter Anette became involved in the management of the company in 1983.

Strategic withdrawal from the tanker market.

While Olsens were so vigorously developing their ferry interests, they were also making another, equally significant strategic move — withdrawing from the tanker market. Before the War, they had owned just one oil tanker, the *Borgny (ii)* of 1929, which was torpedoed and sunk in 1941. In the post-War years, they re-entered the market on a much bigger scale, so that by the beginning of the 1970s British and Norwegian companies within the

The ugly but successful *Borgen (ii)* arrives at Kristiansand after another Skagerak Express crossing from Hirtshals. The rise in traffic on this route led to her being given a drastic reconstruction which greatly enlarged her capacity.
(Bruce Peter collection)

An ugly duckling which did not become a swan. The extent of *Borgen (ii)*'s reconstruction can be seen in this later view of her arriving at Hirtshals. Note the figurehead from a former Olsen ship which has been attached to the front of her superstructure. *(Bruce Peter)*

Olsen group had a dozen large tankers, including three huge 200,000 deadweight tons steam turbine-driven VLCCs (Very Large Crude Carriers) with another one in course of construction. However, the third Fred. Olsen sensed that the tanker market was heading for a serious collapse and between 1970 and 1972 he sold them all. He was not alone in making this judgement but it was a brave move at a time when the market was booming. By 1976, he had been entirely vindicated as other, often very famous, shipowners had large numbers of unemployed tankers lying at moorings in fjords and lochs around the coasts of Norway and Scotland and owed ruinous amounts of money to the banks. It was not until the mid-1980s that Olsen thought the time right to re-enter the tanker market.

Changes on the North Sea.

Turning again to the Olsen passenger shipping interests, the co-operation with the Bergen Line increased in October, 1975 when, as an economy measure made necessary by the huge rise in fuel prices, the two companies co-ordinated their services between Newcastle and Norway under the joint name of Fred. Olsen / Bergen Line. At about the same time, Olsens withdrew the elegant but outdated *Braemar (i)* and sold her to Philippine buyers for use as a floating casino. Henceforth, the *Jupiter* / *Black Watch (ii)* and *Venus* / *Black Prince (ii)* carried both companies' liveries on their yellow funnels during the summer seasons, with the Fred. Olsen flag superimposed on the three narrow silverwhite bands of the Bergen Line. The joint schedule consisted of sailings from Newcastle to Oslo and to Bergen, in both cases via Kristiansand and

Stavanger. These services remained very busy during the summer tourist seasons but eventually it became necessary to withdraw the wintertime sailings.

When the wandering *Bolero* returned from America in 1976, she too was placed on the Fred. Olsen / Bergen Line Norway — Newcastle routes but her extra capacity may have been more than the traffic required and in 1978 she was chartered out again, this time to the Stena Line. For them she flew the Swedish flag while running in their Gothenburg to Kiel service under the name *Scandinavica*. This charter was due to end early in 1982 and, as the time approached, it seemed that she would then be chartered to Brittany Ferries. Indeed, the French company announced that they would call her *Tregor* and they even went so far as to publish a 'doctored' photograph shewing her as she would appear in their livery. Then, at a very late stage, the deal collapsed. Eventually, Olsens sent her, under her old name of *Bolero*, to the Frederikshavn Vaerft in Denmark to be extensively modified in order to make her suitable for their own KDS services between Norway and Denmark. She emerged from this refit with a passenger capacity of 1,600 (872 in cabins and 728 travelling as 'deck passengers') and with space for up to 420 cars. Despite suffering a serious fire in May 1983, she established herself very successfully on her new route. At last, she had found a niche in the Olsen fleet.

The late 1970s and the early 1980s had been a period of turmoil in the ferry services out of Scandinavian ports. In particular, the DFDS company had embarked upon an aggressive expansion, which involved buying up several smaller ferry operators and opening new services —

The versatile *Bolero* motors into Bergen on the 20th September, 1990. She served Olsens well in a variety of capacities, ranging from cruise ship to North Sea and Skagerak ferry. Together with the whole KDS operation, she was sold a few weeks after this photograph was taken. *(Clive Harvey)*

including one between Newcastle and Oslo which syphoned off traffic from the Fred. Olsen / Bergen Line in the prime summer months. It came as a surprise, however, when in October, 1981 it was announced that they had reached an agreement with the Olsen and Bergen companies and, as from the following summer, would be taking over the Fred. Olsen / Bergen Line North Sea services, although still running them under that trade name. They would charter *Venus* and *Jupiter* for the next three summer seasons but in the winter months the ships would, of course, continue to sail to the Canaries for Olsens as *Black Prince (ii)* and *Black Watch (ii)*. The Kristiansand — Harwich summer service would not be resumed in 1982.

At the same time, DFDS bought the *Blenheim (iii)* from Olsens and converted her for the cruise-ferry service with which their newly-formed Scandinavian World Cruises subsidiary was trying to enter the American market. It will be remembered that, unlike her two smaller near-sisters in which the Bergen Line had a large stake, the *Blenheim (iii)* was wholly owned by Olsens. The 1970s had been a troubled time for labour relations in the British shipping industry and Olsens had found the operation of this British-registered and British-crewed ship fraught with problems. In 1979, they announced that they intended to transfer her to the Norwegian flag and run her with Norwegian officers and Portuguese ratings. Predictably, this provoked a strike and, in the end, Olsens agreed to retain the ship's British status and crew. But it may well have been this episode which finally convinced them that there could be no place for the *Blenheim (iii)* in their fleet. When, in October, 1981, it was announced that she had been sold, there was again the inevitable 'industrial

action'. At the time, she was making a cruise from Plymouth to the Canary Islands and for three days the crew delayed her at Gibraltar. When she eventually returned to Plymouth, they staged a sit-in. Finally, however, agreement was reached and the *Blenheim (iii)* was handed over to her new Danish owners. (It should be added that her ill-luck did not end there. In 1984, now called *Scandinavian Sea*, she suffered a devastating fire, which was alleged to have been exacerbated by arson committed by one of the firemen brought in to quell the blaze. Eventually restored, she passed through the hands of various owners until, in 1996, her career was ended by a further fire.)

KDS expansion.

Although the Kristiansand — Harwich service had been abandoned after the 1981 season, Olsens revived it with a short programme of once-a-week sailings in the summer of 1984. These were made by the *Bolero* but the weekly absences from the KDS company's Norway — Denmark schedules which they entailed did not involve any reduction of capacity on those routes. In the past few years, the KDS operation had expanded considerably and at times it had been necessary to charter tonnage from other owners in order to help out. However, the growth of the fleet had since made it possible to maintain the enlarged network of services without bringing in ships from outside. KDS were now running to both Hirtshals and Hansholm, not only from Kristiansand but also from Bergen, Stavanger and Arendal. The wintertime direct sailings from Bergen and Stavanger to Hirtshals were heavily patronised by lorries wishing to avoid the long trek over mountainous and icy roads to Kristiansand as they made their way to Denmark and points south and east. And traffic on the main Kristiansand — Hirtshals route had expanded to such an extent that in 1983 no less than 720,000 passengers were carried.

In 1984, the KDS fleet was augmented by the purchase of a neat-looking 5,288-ton ferry from the Sally Line. Completed in 1974, but re-engined with more powerful diesels in 1982, she had been one of a notable series of similar vessels built by the Jos. L. Meyer yard at Papenburg in Germany. For KDS service, her passenger accommodation was extended and she was called *Bolette (vi)*, a favourite Olsen name. (Bolette Olsen, the wife of the first Petter, was an extremely charitable lady. At Hvitsten you can still see the church which she gave the village in 1903. Also at Hvitsten is the very solid school building given in 1918 by Sofie and the second Fred. Olsen. The local children not only received a free education but the Olsens paid for their books and meals. Among the school's facilities was a large gymnasium and there was a bathroom which was also made available to the adult villagers — men and women on separate days of the week. At that time, this must have been one of the very finest village schools in Norway. To-day, the building houses the Olsen Museum and an office.) In the event, the *Bolette (vi)* did not remain in KDS service for long, being transferred to Morocco in 1988 (see Chapter Nine).

By the time the *Bolette (vi)* was introduced into Skagerak service in 1984, the little *Christian IV* had been withdrawn and was being offered for sale. She had been a stalwart of the Skagerak routes and in a 16 year career had made 12,644 crossings and had carried just over 2 million passengers. Bruce Peter describes her as 'a very pretty and well appointed little ferry, very lovely onboard.' She was eventually sold to Malaysian buyers.

A new flagship.

In 1985, the charter of *Black Watch (ii)* / *Jupiter* to DFDS was extended for a further season but *Black Prince (ii)* / *Venus* was hired for the summer to the newly-formed Norway Line which was taking over the Newcastle — Bergen route from DFDS. The Danish company had been plunged into financial crisis by its over-ambitious expansion. Also in 1985, Olsens made another purchase — the 13,878-ton *Viking Song*, their biggest ferry yet. A product of the Wärtsilä shipyard at Turkü in Finland, she had belonged to the Sally Line who were members of the Viking Line consortium. The ferry services between Finland and Sweden had developed at such a heady pace that the Viking Line partners had now ordered two vessels of over 36,000 tons and, although only five years old, *Viking Song* had been offered for sale. Yet she was a fine ship, built to the highest standards for navigation through ice and with four powerful Wärtsilä-Pielstick diesel engines. It has to be said, though, that her hull, designed for service in the Baltic, proved to be rather less suited to North Sea work and in rough conditions she sometimes found it difficult to maintain her scheduled speed. Nevertheless, in other respects she proved to be an extremely good vessel.

She could carry over 2,000 passengers, about half of them in cabin accommodation, and she provided them with facilities which, at that time, were quite outstanding for a ferry. Olsens took delivery of her in May, called her *Braemar (ii)* and sent her to the Blohm & Voss yard at Hamburg for a refit which increased her gross tonnage to 14,623 and from which she emerged with even better passenger facilities, including a two deck-high 'tropical garden'. Writing in *Ships Monthly*, the maritime journalist Russell Plummer described this room as 'one of the most remarkable facilities I have seen in a vessel of this type. Grape vines and exotic plants help to create a unique atmosphere and from the glass-roofed upper area, double-width stairs lead down to the even larger lower level with the whole area transformed by night into a disco with a stunning light show and array of special effects.' Elsewhere, 'somewhat more refined dance music is provided by a full orchestra'. According to Plummer, the *Braemar (ii)* had 'the highest quality accommodation yet seen on a North Sea service'. Although new entrants to the Olsen fleets were no longer being given bow decorations, the old tradition was not entirely forgotten and, above the ramp at her stem, the *Braemar (ii)* carried the figurehead which had once adorned the bow of the cargo ship *Bergerac*, whilst a sculpture from *Braemar (i)* was also

By the 1980s, new Olsen ships were no longer being given figureheads but some of those which had been worn by earlier vessels were recycled on board the ferries and cruise ships. Here the one from the freighter *Biri (ii)* decorates *Bolero*'s sun deck. (*Bruce Peter collection*)

The figurehead from the bow of the cargo ship *Bergerac* was now affixed above the ramp at the stern of the substantial former Finnish ferry which joined the KDS fleet as *Braemar (ii)* in 1985. *(Bruce Peter)*

displayed on board. The new ship's hull was painted white rather than the usual Fred. Olsen grey and this livery gradually spread throughout the whole ferry fleet.

Olsen/KDS ferries were expected to earn their keep by running intensive schedules and in that first summer season *Braemar (ii)*'s weekly Harwich voyages were interspersed with Skagerak crossings. Thereafter, her Harwich service became a year-round affair but now from Oslo rather than Kristiansand and with a call at Hirtshals. In between these North Sea crossings, the *Braemar (ii)* made regular Oslo — Hirtshals sailings. In bringing such a splendid ship into service from the Norwegian capital, Olsens were mounting a determined challenge to the other operators who were already running between there and Danish ports. For two years, the *Bolero* took over the brief Kristiansand — Harwich summer seasons, but it would seem that there was insufficient traffic to support two services between southern Norway and Britain and the sailings from Kristiansand were abandoned.

An abortive project.

In 1988, Olsens began planning a new 26,000-ton 'mega-ferry' to be given the hopeful name of *Bonanza (iii)*. The origins of this vessel were somewhat unusual. She was one of four overnight ferries which had been ordered from Polish builders by the Stena Line of Gothenburg as long ago as 1979. The shipyard workers of Gdansk and Gdynia were, of course, at the forefront of the brave Polish

struggle for independence from Soviet domination in the 1980s but in the process they frequently 'downed tools' and disrupted production. By 1986, only two of the four ships had been delivered and Stena's patience finally ran out. They cancelled the orders for the remaining pair. The third vessel had been launched in 1984 without name or ceremony (although apparently the original intention had been to call her *Stena Baltica*) and she lay, engined but otherwise unfinished, until 1988. Olsens saw an opportunity and bought her through a London finance company. They announced plans to send her to the Bremer Vulcan yard at Vegesack for completion as by far the largest ferry yet to run on the Kristiansand — Hirtshals route. However, in the event, she remained laid-up in Poland until the following January, when it became known that Olsens had sold her to the Cretan line ANEK. It was rumoured that they had made a pleasant profit on the transaction. Her new owners had her towed to Perama, near Piraeus, where she was completed. She entered their service as *Kydon II*, later being renamed *El. Venizelos*.

A few months later in 1989, Olsens found a suitable replacement. They bought the 14,982-ton *Olau Britannia*, one of two sisters built in Germany in 1981-82, which (although they had recently been sold to the Swedish firm of Nordström & Thulin) were still running between the Kentish port of Sheerness and Vlissingen in The Netherlands for their original owners, the Olau Line. With her short bow and with her six decks of superstructure

This aerial view of the *Braemar (ii)* at sea clearly shews the bluff shape of her bow, more suited to the Baltic service for which she had been built than for the North Sea crossings which she now made.
(Postcard, Bruce Peter collection)

The *Braemar (ii)* was remarkable for the scope and the decoration of her interiors. Without a doubt, she offered her passengers more and better facilities than any other ferry on the North Sea routes when Olsens introduced her in 1985. *(Postcard, John Sutherland collection)*

spreading along almost her entire length, the *Olau Britannia* was a blockish, bulky-looking ship but during her years with Olau she had gained an excellent reputation. Facilities on board included not only a swimming pool but also a solarium, a gymnasium and saunas and her passenger accommodation was divided vertically, with all cabins at the forward end of the ship, well away from the noise of the public rooms further aft. The *Olau Britannia* remained with the Olau Line until the new vessel which was to replace her arrived in May, 1990. Once handed over to Olsens, she was given the famous old name of *Bayard (viii)*. Although already very well furnished — if in a somewhat subdued style — she now received a thorough refurbishment which included the provision of additional cabins. She entered service for Olsens in June, 1990.

Meanwhile, the Olsen ferry services were going through a rather restless phase. In August, 1989, the intermittent flirtation with the port of Harwich finally ended when the *Braemar (ii)*'s crossings from Oslo and Hirtshals were switched to Newcastle (in fact, to Olsens' traditional terminal at North Shields). This was a shorter voyage and therefore more economical in fuel, and it also attracted many Norwegian shoppers who were taken by bus to the MetroCentre at Gateshead, a few miles out of Newcastle, which is reputed to be the largest shopping and leisure centre in Europe. There, in its 330 shops, they eagerly took advantage of prices which were usually much less expensive than those at home.

In 1990, Olsens introduced a summertime-only link between Newcastle and the western Norwegian ports of Molde, Måløy, Alesund and Bergen, which brought them into direct competition with Norway Line (by now part of the Kosmos group). This new service was entrusted to the *Bolero* which had been extensively refurbished for the purpose and had 85 extra cabins built into part of her car deck. In addition to catering for normal traffic, these sailings could be marketed in Britain as mini-cruises to a very beautiful part of Norway. As usual, the ships were

intensively used and, in between their sailings on the Norway — England routes, both the *Bolero* and the *Braemar (ii)* contributed to the KDS Norway to Denmark schedules. Norway Line was in an equally competitive mood and now tried to break into the Norway — Denmark trade by including a call at Esbjerg in its sailings between Bergen, Stavanger and the Tyne.

Strategic withdrawal.

Then, suddenly, Olsens executed another strategic turn— they withdrew from the ferry business. The first hint of this had come in September, 1990, when it was announced that the splendid *Braemar (ii)* was to be sold to the Baltic Shipping Co. of Leningrad. In fact, like several of the state-owned Soviet shipping companies, this concern was in financial difficulties and the sale fell through. However, in the end the ship was sold to a Cypriot-registered concern and entered the Baltic company's service between Leningrad and Stockholm as the *Anna Karenina*.

Then, in December, came the surprise announcement that the Olsen/KDS North Sea and Skagerak services, together with the *Bolero*, *Borgen (ii)* and *Bayard (viii)*, had been sold for the equivalent of about £104 million to Color Line. This was a new company only recently formed by the Kosmos group to amalgamate Norway Line and the Jahre Line. The actual transfer of ownership took place on the 15th December, marked on board the ships with a ceremonial lowering of the Fred. Olsen colours and the raising of the Color Line flag.

By now, Olsens had turned their attention to other fields. In the mid-1970s, they had entered the North Sea oil rig business; in 1986, they had returned to the tanker market under the trade name Knock Tankers; in 1989, they bought a controlling interest in the Harland & Wolff shipyard in Belfast; they were developing ferry services in the Canary Islands and to Morocco (see Chapter Nine); and, of course, there were the cruises run by *Black Prince (ii)* which we shall discuss in the Chapter Ten.

The German-built *Bayard (viii)* made a good impression during her brief spell as a member of the KDS fleet before Olsens sold their North Sea and Skagerak ferry interests to other Norwegian owners in 1990. *(Frank Heine, John Sutherland collection)*

9.

Enterprise in the Canaries and in Morocco

CANARY ISLANDS.

Olsen family involvement in the Canary Islands dates back to the early years of the twentieth century when the second Fred. Olsen bought a parcel of agricultural land on La Gomera. It was in 1920, however, that he started to run ships between the islands and northern Europe, carrying tomatoes and other produce in their heavily ventilated holds. Shortly afterwards he acquired a controlling interest in the Otto Thoresen fleet, which was already well established on the route. Later, when *Black Watch (ii)* and *Black Prince (ii)* began bringing cruise passengers and other visitors to the islands in the mid-1960s, the Fred. Olsen services became even more important to the Canaries. This has not gone unrecognised – there are streets named Avenida Fred. Olsen (Fred. Olsen Avenue) not only in San Sebastian de la Gomera but also in Arecife on the island of Lanzarote; and for a long time a certificate acknowledging her contribution to the islands' economy was prominently displayed on board *Black Prince (ii)*. To-day, the family interests in the Canaries are presided over by Fred. Olsen, Jr., (the fourth Fred. Olsen).

La Gomera is one of the smaller, quieter islands and, among much else, the family own the luxurious Hotel Jardin Tecina, the Restaurante Las Rosas, an 18-hole golf course and a residential development called the Pueblo Don Thomas. In the 1970s, they set up a Spanish-registered company, Ferry Gomera S.A., which on the 8th July, 1974 started running a vehicle and passenger service linking San Sebastian de la Gomera with Los Cristianos on

the neighbouring island of Tenerife. To make this crossing of about 20 miles, they had ordered a small ferry from the Trondheims Mekaniske Verksted in Norway. Of just 887 gross tons and with her engines aft, she could carry 399 deck passengers. In addition to her car deck, she had a limited amount of refrigerated space which enabled her to carry fruit. Registered in San Sebastian de la Gomera, she was called *Benchijigua (i)* – suitably, since that is a very scenic part of the island and also conforms to the Olsen tradition of giving their ships names beginning with the letter 'B'. Over the years, *Benchijigua* has come to be regarded as a particularly prestigious name and is usually borne by the biggest and fastest newcomer to Olsens' Canary Islands fleet.

That very first *Benchijigua* was, however, a modest little ship. She maintained the service single-handedly for six years but by 1980 traffic had increased sufficiently to require a larger vessel. Olsens found her within their own fleet: the *Bonanza (ii)* of 1972, one of the pair of versatile vessels which, as we saw in Chapter Eight, had been built for part-time use in the KDS Skagerak Express ferry service. She was no stranger to the Canary Islands, however, as she was also designed for rapid out-of-season conversion into a refrigerated 'fruiter'. At 2,699 gross tons and able to carry 750 deck passengers and 200 cars (or up to 16 lorries and a lesser number of cars), she was both a larger and a faster ship than the *Benchijigua (i)*. She now took not only the place, but also the name, of that tiny pioneer, which became the *Betancuria (ii)* before eventually being sold to Icelandic owners.

The 'new' *Benchijigua (ii)* (ex-*Bonanza (ii)*) remained

Benchijigua (i), the modest vessel which initiated the local Ferry Gomera service in 1974. Few would then have dared to forecast that she would be the forerunner of the present-day Fred. Olsen Express network of fast ferry services round the Canary Islands. (*Bruce Peter collection*)

Bajamar (iii) had started life as the KDS ferry *Bonanza (ii)* which also worked in the Canaries fruit trade. Later, she came to Ferry Gomera as *Benchijigua (ii)* before becoming one of the stalwarts of the Lineas Fred. Olsen services. *(Alex Duncan, Newall-Dunn collection)*

Ferry Gomera's sole vessel for another nine years, until 1989, when she was joined by the *Betancuria (iii)*. This small passenger and car ferry (681 gross tons) was also Norwegian-built, having come from the Storviks Mekaniske Verksted shipyard in 1966 as the Stavangerske Dampskibsselskab's *Tungenes* and she was a typical example of a whole generation of small Scandinavian ships of this sort. By the time she was bought by Olsens, she had already passed through the hands of Icelandic and German owners. Ferry Gomera (and their successor company) kept her until 1995, when they sold her to a Spanish-owned company for Mediterranean service as the *Ciudad de Melilla*.

Moving into a bigger league.

During those first two decades, Ferry Gomera was merely a small local company serving a rather unimportant island. There was little indication that it would one day burst forth as a vigorous and innovative competitor to the two established operators of ferry services in the Canaries, Trasmediterránea and Naviera Armas. However, in 1993 these wider ambitions led to the dropping of the name Ferry Gomera and the appearance of a new corporate title, Lineas Fred. Olsen, painted in large letters along the ships' sides. To-day, the line not only provides a link between San Sebastian de la Gomera and Los Cristianos but also operates other routes between Los Cristianos and Santa

Another small vessel, *Betancuria (iii)*, joined the Ferry Gomera (later Lineas Fred. Olsen) fleet in 1989. It will seen that the Fred. Olsen flag on her dummy funnel is in the Spanish national colours of red and yellow. *(Newall-Dunn collection)*

The unprepossessing but hard-working *Buganvilla*, German-built and formerly Swedish-owned, came to Ferry Gomera in 1992. The following year, the new title Lineas Fred. Olsen was adopted for the expanding ferry operations in the Canaries. *(Postcard, author's collection)*

Cruz de la Palma; Los Cristianos and La Estaca (on the small island of El Hierro); Santa Cruz de Tenerife and Agaete (on Gran Canaria); and Lanzarote and Corralejo (on the island of Fuerteventura).

A third ship had been added to the fleet in 1992. She was the *Buganvilla*, a German-built 2,452-tonner which dated back to 1968. As the Swedish *Betula*, she had been one of the ferries which ran the busy shuttle service across the Øresund between Helsingborg and Helsingør, often carrying large numbers of thirsty Swedes heading for the opposite shore, where they could buy cheap Danish alcohol. With both a bow door and a ramp leading onto her open stern deck, she could house up to 105 cars in addition to 800 passengers. It has to be said that, with her short bow and bulky superstructure, she had a rather foreshortened appearance. In fact, extra superstructure had been added during a rebuilding in 1982, during which she had also been re-engined. She served Lineas Fred. Olsen well for ten years, mainly on their new service linking Lanzarote and Corralejo. Then, in 2002, she was sold to owners in the Cape Verde Islands where, by coincidence, she ran in conjunction with another ex-Fred. Olsen ferry, the former *Christian IV* of the KDS Skagerak Express service.

The line's ambitious expansion plans led to further acquisitions in 1994 as a result of which two much bigger ferries joined the fleet. In the process, the faithful *Benchijigua (ii)* gave up her name to one of them and became the *Bajamar (iii)*. The 'new' *Benchijigua (iii)* was a substantial but good-looking 8,531-tonner which had been completed in 1974 by the Schichau-Unterweser yard in Bremerhaven as the *Djursland II* (later simply *Djursland*). Her original owners ran a service linking the Danish ports of Grenaa and Hundested and, although she had subsequently changed hands twice, she had remained on this route and had retained her name. She could carry 370 cars on her two vehicle decks and no less than 1,500 passengers (112 of them in cabins). She had been designed by the Knud E. Hansen company but had a rather more conservative appearance than many of the ships shaped in that office. After buying her, Lineas Fred. Olsen had her refurbished at Southampton before employing her mainly on the routes out of Los Cristianos.

The other major acquisition in 1994 was the 9,735-ton *Bañaderos (iii)*, which had long been familiar to many British passengers as Townsend Thoresen's *Viking Voyager* of 1976 and later as P&O Ferries' *Pride of Cherbourg*. With hardly a curve to be seen anywhere and lacking any pretence of elegance, she was one of a series of functional but useful ferries which the Aalborg yard in Denmark had built for the Townsend Thoresen company. (Although British, this concern was partly of Norwegian origin. In fact, the Thoresen involvement came from the same family whose 'fruiter' fleet had joined the Fred. Olsen empire in the early 1920s.) The *Bañaderos (iii)* could carry 1,286 passengers (86 in cabins) and 275 cars and had a sophisticated and quite speedy three-engined, triple-screw propulsion system.

With the purchase of these capacious – if already somewhat mature – vessels, Lineas Fred. Olsen were able to establish themselves as major ferry operators around the Canary Islands. Intriguingly, however, they were turning their minds to providing much speedier services. Their third purchase in 1994 was a small catamaran hovercraft (officially described in *Lloyd's Register* as an air cushion ferry). She was said to have a service speed of no less than 46 knots (as compared to the 17 knots and 21 knots of the *Benchijigua (iii)* and *Bañaderos (iii)*) and was one of a class designed by Cirrus International of Bergen and built by the Brødrene Aa Batbyggeri (i.e.: Aa Brothers Boatyard). Of reinforced plastic construction, she could carry 300 passengers, all in aircraft-type seats. When she came out

In the mid-1990s, Lineas Fred. Olsen had a somewhat eclectic fleet of former European ferries, the largest of which was *Bañaderos (iii)*, an uncompromisingly functional-looking ex-Townsend Thoresen vessel, seen here at Tenerife in April, 1999. *(Clive Harvey)*

as the *Sant' Agata* in 1989, her Norwegian owners chartered her to the British operators of a new Cowes Express service linking Southampton and East Cowes in the Isle of Wight. Mechanical, and possibly financial, problems led to the closure of the service in 1990 and, although there was an attempt to revive it, with the former *Sant' Agata* now called *Wight King*, it did not last long. In 1994, the vessel was bought by Lineas Fred. Olsen and, after a refit at Poole, she entered their service as the *Bahia Express*. In the end, they seem to have decided that other technology was preferable to that of the hovercraft and maybe that she was too small to be economic. At any rate, they sold her to owners based in Kuwait in 1997.

Buques Rapidos – fast ferries.

In 1999, a new Olsen company named Canaria de Buques Rapidos, SA, again Spanish-registered, took delivery of the first two of three catamarans which it had ordered from Incat Australia of Hobart in Tasmania, one of two Australian builders who have come to dominate the market for large craft of this kind. The third member of the trio was completed early the following year. The structures of these twin-hulled craft are 96 metres long (i.e.: 315 feet) and are built of aluminium alloy. The first of the three is called *Bonanza Express*, has a gross tonnage of 5,199 and can carry 230 cars (or an equivalent number of cars and lorries or buses) on her capacious vehicle deck, which is loaded over the stern. She can accommodate 735

passengers, has comfortable Club Class and Gold Class lounges, a bar-cafeteria and a children's play room. With her four powerful V20-cylinder Ruston engines, she can maintain a service speed of 38 knots so that she is able to make the long crossing from Los Cristianos to Puerto de la Estaca on the island of El Hierro in about two hours. She also makes some voyages on the Los Cristianos – San Sebastian de la Gomera route. Free bus connections are provided across the island of Tenerife between Los Cristianos and the capital city of Santa Cruz de Tenerife.

In 2001, the *Bonanza Express* was sent to the other side of the Atlantic so that Olsens could experiment with a fast service between Miami and, it was hoped, Nassau in the Bahamas. But the Bahamian authorities refused to allow her to run into the port of Nassau, insisting that she should go to Freeport instead. This proved to be uneconomic and the service was closed after just four months, whereupon the *Bonanza Express* returned home to the Canaries.

The second of these initial catamarans was at first called the *Bentayga Express*. Although of the same length as the *Bonanza Express*, she is bigger at 6,344 gross tons and can carry 871 passengers and up to 300 cars. She has four Caterpillar V18-cylinder engines. In 2004, when one of her sisters was given the rather similar name of *Bentago Express* (see below), she became the *Bencomo Express* in order to avoid confusion. (This prompts the irreverent thought that, with so many ships bearing similar or

Ferry services between the Canary Islands were transformed by the arrival of Fred. Olsen Express's speedy, Australian-built catamarans in 1999 and 2000. Here *Bentago Express* pauses between crossings at Agaete on Gran Canaria. *(John Sutherland)*

identical names in the various Olsen fleets over the years, confusion is hard to avoid – at least for the shipping historian.) In 2007, the *Bencomo Express* was running on the hour-long crossing between Santa Cruz de Tenerife and Agaete in partnership with the *Bentago Express*. Free bus connections are offered at Agaete to and from Las Palmas de Gran Canaria.

The final member of the trio was for some years called the *Benchijigua Express* but in 2004 she ceded that prestigious name to a new and bigger craft and so became the *Bentago Express*. She too is Caterpillar-powered and she has a passenger capacity of 941. The sight of these futuristic-looking catamarans accelerating out of port and disappearing over the horizon at high speed, with their water jets spouting plumes of foam at the stern, is tremendously exciting and has all the éclat to be expected of a genuine express service. In their brochures, Fred. Olsen Express claim to be Tu Mejor Compañía (i.e.: Your Best Company) and describe their service as Fácil, Cómodo y Económico (Convenient, Comfortable and Inexpensive).

Bonanza Express **features on the cover of a 2006 timetable for the route between Los Cristianos on Tenerife and the island of El Hierro. The Fred. Olsen Express services now carry about 3 million passengers per annum.** *(Author's collection)*

The hugely impressive trimaran *Benchijigua Express (ii)*, introduced in 2005, is the largest multi-hulled vessel in the World and can maintain a service speed of no less than 40 knots. She is said to have cost $45 million. *(Author)*

Benchijigua Express (ii) makes one of her regular arrivals at San Sebastian de la Gomera. This stern view gives an indication of the size of her capacious vehicle deck which can accommodate up to 341 cars. *(John Sutherland)*

In 2003, a smaller catamaran, the *Bocayna Express*, arrived from different Australian builders, Austal Ships of Fremantle. With a gross tonnage of 2,578, four Paxman engines and a capacity of 450 passengers and 69 cars, she was allocated to the short 20-minute crossing between Lanzarote and Corralejo, on which she replaced the orthodox ferry *Buganvilla*.

The advent of the catamarans, in fact, led to the departure of most of the ferry fleet. The *Benchijigua (iii)* was at first renamed *Betancuria (iv)* but in 2002 she was sold to Egyptian owners who called her *Sara 1*. She will re-appear later in this chapter when we deal with group's Moroccan operations. The *Bajamar (iii)* was to have gone to Filippino owners in 2001 but, with the ship already renamed *Blessed Mother*, the sale fell through and she lay idle for two years with no owners specified in *Lloyd's Register*. She emerged from this limbo existence in 2003 when she was bought by owners in the Azores who have used her for inter-island service. The *Bañaderos* hung on until 2005, latterly under the name *Barlovento*, but she was then superseded by an amazing new vessel and was sold to a Greek company for use in the Aegean.

The remarkable new craft, which of course is called *Benchijigua Express (ii)*, is a trimaran rather than a catamaran. At 126.7 metres (415 feet) and 8,000 gross tons, she is the biggest multi-hulled ship in the World and is said to be the largest all-aluminium structure. She can carry a maximum of 341 cars (or alternatively 600 lineal metres of freight vehicles and 123 cars) and 1,291 passengers, who enjoy even better facilities than those on the catamarans. Her four MTU 20-cylinder engines power her along at up to 40 knots and she runs on both the Los Cristianos – Santa Cruz de la Palma and the Los Cristianos – San Sebastian de la Gomera routes. Said to have cost $45 million, she was built by Austal Ships and attracted a great deal of attention at the time. Indeed, on her lengthy, and very speedy, delivery voyage to the Canaries she carried a large number of U.S. naval personnel who were there specifically to observe her performance.

It will be interesting to see how Lineas Fred. Olsen develops further, having already made a huge difference to travel and transport around the Canary Islands. Just how great the effect has been can be seen from the figures. In its first half-year, in 1974, Ferry Gomera's little *Benchijigua (i)* carried just 25,000 passengers. By 2003, the Fred. Olsen fleet in the Canary Islands was carrying 2,700,000 passengers, 400,000 cars and more than 150,000 trucks per annum.

MOROCCO.

Over the years, Fred. Olsen ships often visited Moroccan ports but in 1984 the family became more involved in the trade to and from this North African kingdom, having set up the Compagnie Maritime Maroco-Norvégienne (usually known as Comarit) in co-operation with local interests. Its headquarters were initially in Casablanca but were later transferred to Tangiers. The new company's first ship was the former *Buenavista (ii)* of 3,282 gross tons. As we saw in Chapter Eight, she had been built in 1971 for the Skagerak Express car, train and passenger ferry service but with a design so adaptable that she could also serve as a refrigerated 'fruiter' on Olsens' Canaries run. In 1977, she had passed to a Dutch company who chartered her back to Fred. Olsen & Co. and had latterly been running as a ro-ro freighter between Casablanca and Agadir on the Atlantic coast of Morocco and several Northern European ports. When the new Comarit company acquired her in early in 1984, they hoisted the Moroccan flag and called her *Bismillah (iii)*. Although a traditional Olsen name, this was very suitable

The long-serving *Bismillah (iii)*, seen here arriving at Algeciras, was the pioneer which established the Comarit services between Morocco and Spain in 1984. She had started life as the versatile KDS ferry *Buenavista (ii)*. *(Bruce Peter collection)*

Another ferry which saw service in the KDS Skagerak Express service before coming to Morocco is the *Boughaz* (ex-*Bolette (vi)*). In this photograph, taken at Gibraltar in March, 1996, it will be seen that by then sponsons had been added along the sides of her hull. *(Tony Davis)*

A further view of *Boughaz*, this time at Algeciras in 2007. By now, at 5,000 gross tons, she is the smallest vessel in the Comarit / Lineas Maritimas Europeas fleet, increasing traffic having necessitated the purchase of larger ships. *(Bruce Peter)*

Although the majority of their passengers are more interested in travelling cheaply than in comfort, the Comarit ships do have a certain amount of pleasant accommodation for better-off clients, as illustrated by *Boughaz*'s Club Lounge. *(Bruce Peter)*

as it is, in fact, a Muslim blessing, variously translated as 'In the name of Allah' or 'By the will of Allah'. This name was now painted in both Arabic and Roman script on the ship's bow and stern.

New ferry services.

Comarit kept the *Bismillah (iii)* on the Morocco – Europe run in the winter months, sometimes sending her as far north as Helsinki, but in the Summer they used her for a new Morocco – Spain passenger and vehicle ferry service. In that first 1984 season she ran between Tangiers and Malaga but the following year she was switched to a shorter Tangiers – Algeciras route on which she remained for most of her long career with Comarit. This is a two-hour crossing and the *Bismillah (iii)* was intensively used,

shuttling backwards and forwards at frequent intervals. As on most of the routes between North Africa and Europe, many of her passengers were poor migrants. Ships in this trade have to endure some very hard wear but high speed is not important. It may be for these reasons that, whereas Olsens have upgraded their services in the Canaries with new and very modern fast craft, they have remained content to use conventional ferries for their Moroccan operation.

By 1988, a second ship was already needed to cope with the growth in traffic and the *Bolette (vi)*, the smart German-built 5,286-ton ferry which had been running in the Skagerak Express service for the last four years (see Chapter Eight), was accordingly transferred to Comarit. They called her *Boughaz*.

The acquisition of the former Danish ferry *Banasa* in 1996, marked a further stage in the development of the Comarit fleet. Since this picture was taken as she arrived at Algeciras on the 8th August, 1998, she has been given sponsons and a 'duck-tail' stern. *(Tony Davis)*

Together, the *Bismillah (iii)* and the *Boughaz* maintained a two-ship operation between Tangiers and Algeciras until 1996, when they were joined by the *Banassa*, whose name was quickly amended to *Banasa*. This vessel, a product of the Helsingør shipyard, had started life in 1975 as the *Mette Mols* belonging to a DFDS subsidiary which ran a ferry service within the Danish archipelago. Having been built for a short domestic route, she has very few cabins but can carry over 1,600 passengers. With access through bow, side and stern doors, her decks can accommodate up to 420 cars or an equivalent number of cars, lorries and trailers. When she joined the Comarit fleet in 1996, she was, at 11,668 gross tons, by far its biggest member yet but she has since been surpassed in size by later comers, an indication of how the company's trade has developed. By the early 2000s, the *Banasa* was beginning to suffer mechanical problems and so, at the end of the 2003 season, she was re-engined with new and more powerful MAN/Burmeister & Wain diesels. In fact, the changes went beyond this and the famous Blohm & Voss shipyard in Hamburg brought her into compliance with the latest stability regulations by adding side sponsons. At the same time, they constructed a 'duck tail' at the stern (a flared skirt at the waterline, intended to give a smoother ride and to improve fuel consumption). Following these expensive modifications, the *Banasa* returned to the Tangiers – Algeciras run.

Banasa provides pleasant and comfortable surroundings for her better-off passengers on the two-hour crossing between Tangiers and Algeciras. Here we see the Observation Lounge and the Restaurant. *(Bruce Peter)*

An atmospheric nocturnal view of *Banasa*'s boat deck. *(Bruce Peter)*

Berkane, a former French ferry, has the largest capacity of any ship in the Comarit fleet and is also the fastest. Although she has mainly been used on the long Nador — Almeria route, she is pictured here at Algeciras. *(Bruce Peter)*

New routes and more ships.

In recent years, Olsens' interests in the ferry trades in this area have been divided between the Comarit company and a Spanish-registered subsidiary called Lineas Maritimas Europeas which took over the *Boughaz*. However, both firms work so closely together and their services are so integrated that to the outsider they form a single entity, even though the ships carry different company names on their hulls.

A number of concerns of varied ownership and nationality are involved in the intense operation of ferries between Morocco and ports in Spain and France. On the route between Tangiers and Algeciras, Comarit and its subsidiary company were for some years members of a 'pool' of seven operators who between them ran an hourly service during the peak season. Comarit's operations have expanded considerably and they now participate with two other companies in another service between Morocco and Spain, this time between Nador in eastern Morocco and Almeria. In addition, they now operate on the much longer route between Nador and the French port of Sète and for a time they had a service between Al Hoceima and Almeria.

As their operations expanded, and with their existing three ships mostly occupied in the main Tangiers – Algeciras service, it became necessary for them to add to

their fleet. In 2002, they purchased a powerful French ferry called *Napoléon* – aptly named since she had been one of the stalwarts of the routes linking France and Corsica. This 20,079-ton ship, now called *Berkane*, had been completed by the Dubigeon-Normandie yard in 1976 and has something of the look of a conventional ocean liner – until, that is, one notices her flat ferry stern with its ramp-type door. Access to her vehicle decks, which can hold up to 435 cars and lorries, is also through both bow and side doors. She can carry up to 2,102 passengers, of whom 378 can be accommodated in cabins. She is a fast ship, her two powerful V18-cylinder Pielstick engines giving her a service speed of up to 24.6 knots, which is useful on the long run between Nador and Almeria, on which she has been mainly employed.

The following year, the *Liberté*, another Dubigeon-built former French Corsican ferry, joined the Comarit fleet and was renamed *Biladi*. She now established the new service to Sète. An 18,913-tonner, she has cabin accommodation for 356 passengers out of a total complement of up to 1,812. She can carry up to 500 cars and lorries. Although she too is powered by twin V18-cylinder Pielsticks, she is not as quick a ship as the *Berkane* and has a service speed of 20.7 knots.

In 2003, an additional vessel was needed for the new service between Al Hoceima and Almeria. This time, she

Another ferry acquired from the French, who had used her on their Corsican routes, the *Biladi* has been somewhat modified by Comarit, particularly at the stern. This picture captures her at Tangiers on the 23rd May, 2007. *(Bruce Peter)*

The Egyptian *Sara 1*, seen in Tangiers on the 23rd May, 2007, was once owned by Lineas Fred. Olsen and was a familiar sight around the Canary Islands. Here, however, she is under charter to the Olsen controlled Lineas Maritimas Europeas for service between Morocco and Spain. *(Bruce Peter)*

was chartered rather than bought. She was, though, a former Lineas Fred. Olsen vessel, the *Betancuria (iv)* which, it may be remembered, had once been the *Benchijigua (iii)*. She had been sold in 2002 to the Egyptian company El Salam Shipping, who called her *Sara* 1 (8,531 gross tons) and briefly ran her in the Red Sea. Within months, however, they had chartered her to the Lineas Maritimas Europeas and, at the time of writing, she remains with them.

2006 saw the departure of a faithful servant. The *Bismillah (iii)* was now 35 years old and had been a very useful and popular ship, at first as the *Buenavista (ii)* in the KDS Skagerak Express service and on the Fred. Olsen 'fruiter' run from the Canaries to northern Europe; and

later, under her present name, she had been the Comarit company's pioneer vessel, remaining with them for 22 years. Latterly, she had been in regular service only during the summer months but had acted as the reserve ship for the rest of the year. New and even more stringent stability regulations now meant that if she was to continue sailing on an international route, she would require modifications which, given her age, would be too costly to justify. She could still sail in coastal waters, however, and she was therefore sold to a Mexican company who renamed her *El Arcangel*. Her departure precipitated the transfer of the chartered *Sara 1* to the Tangiers – Algeciras run and the abandonment of the Al Hoceima – Almeria service.

Changing fashions in publicity material

R. M. S. Scotland, Outward Bound, Grangemouth.

For many years, coloured images were produced by tinting black and white photographs. This one portrays the Christiania — Grangemouth steamer *Scotland (ii)*, whose brief career lasted only from 1904 until 1911. *(Postcard, Ambrose Greenway collection)*

Publicity material produced for shipping companies by commercial artists often gave an exaggeratedly imposing impression of their ships. However, this painting of *Brabant (iii)* in her funnel-less days before 1937 gives a fairly accurate view of her. *(Postcard, Ambrose Greenway collection)*

The designer of this 1938 brochure for the new Oslo — Tyne liner *Black Prince (i)* chose to decorate the cover with a portrayal of her striking figurehead rather than one of the ship herself. A nautical touch was added by the use of the Fred. Olsen flag. *(Newall-Dunn collection)*

By contrast, this attractive brochure advertising Olsens' Oslo — Antwerp service in 1951 features an uncomplicated but fairly accurate aerial image of *Brabant (iii)*. It is very typical of the style of the period.
(John Sutherland collection)

The cover of the booklet produced to mark the introduction of the ultra-streamlined *Braemar (i)* in 1953 bore this wonderfully stylish portrayal of her unusual combined funnel and mast and her rounded solarium.
(John Sutherland collection)

menu ...
M·S BRAEMAR

To this day, menus often carry colourful artwork on their covers. This one from the Tyne — Oslo liner *Braemar (i)* suitably combined tourist's-eye views of picturesque aspects of British and Norwegian life. *(Author's collection)*

North Pacific
via Panama Canal

by FRED. OLSEN *Line*

A 1960 brochure used this tranquil scene to attract leisured passengers to the quiet pleasures of travel in the passenger quarters of the cargo liners on the long run between Europe and the North Pacific via the Panama Canal.
(John Sutherland collection)

In the early 1980s, cruise brochures such as this one promoting Fred. Olsen's voyages to Madeira and the Canary Islands still tended to focus on the ships themselves. To-day, there is much more emphasis on the destinations and on selling the brand.
(Author's collection)

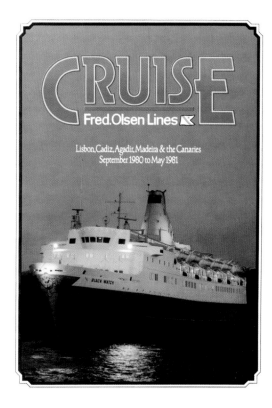

CRUISE
Fred. Olsen Lines
Lisbon, Cadiz, Agadir, Madeira & the Canaries
September 1980 to May 1981

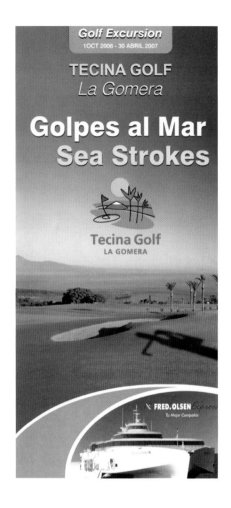

A bright, modern leaflet published in Spanish and English in 2006 advertises the Tecina golf course on La Gomera and the Fred. Olsen Express fast ferry service which provides a convenient link to the island. *(Author's collection)*

A sunlit postcard view of the spectacular Hotel Jardin Tecina on La Gomera. The hotel is one of a number of Olsen enterprises on the island, where the family have been established for about a century. *(Postcard, John Sutherland collection)*

Tusenfryd (A Thousand Joys) is an Olsen-owned pleasure park some miles out of Oslo. This postcard view, with its blue sky and fresh, open air feeling as well as its exciting rides, does indeed seem to offer many different kinds of pleasure. *(Postcard, John Sutherland collection)*

10.
Black Prince (ii) Reborn

The agreement between Fred. Olsen and the Bergen Line under which they shared the ownership of *Black Watch (ii)* / *Jupiter*, and eventually also *Black Prince (ii)* / *Venus*, was intended to last for twenty years and it therefore expired in 1986. As we have seen in a previous chapter, the two companies had in 1982 handed on their North Sea ferry services to the Danish company DFDS, which immediately took both ships on charter. There was further change in 1985 when the Danes abandoned the Bergen to Newcastle service and a new company, Norway Line, moved in to fill the gap. Soon afterwards, Norway Line was acquired by the Kosmos group which had also recently taken over the Bergen Line.

At the end of the 1986 summer season, with the Olsen / Bergen agreement due to terminate, this complicated financial gavotte culminated in the two ships changing ownership. The Kosmos group bought out the Olsen interest in *Black Watch (ii)* / *Jupiter*, while Olsens purchased the Kosmos share in *Black Prince (ii)* / *Venus*. Olsens thus became her sole owners. Whereas the *Jupiter*

continued in service as a Norway Line ferry (but her wintertime Canary Islands sailings for Olsens were discontinued), there were very different plans for *Black Prince (ii)*. In October, 1986, Olsens sent her to the Turkü yard of the Finnish shipbuilders Wärtsilä for conversion into a full-time cruise ship at a cost of about $15 million. In one sense, it was ironic that it should be *Black Prince (ii)* which would be used for cruising since Olsens intended to concentrate on the British market and *Black Watch (ii)* had in recent years been better known among British passengers.

Olsens were, of course, no strangers to the cruise market – for years they had been selling their winter voyages to Madeira and the Canaries as round trips to the sun; and *Black Watch (ii)*, *Black Prince (ii)* and *Blenheim (iii)* had all made occasional more far-ranging cruises. Now, however, a more comprehensive programme was planned, still with many visits to the Atlantic islands but also with trips to the Mediterranean, Norway and the Baltic. The aim was to attract a wider range of passengers

Black Prince (ii) **departs from Southampton on the 28th February, 1987 at the start of her first voyage of her new career as a full-time cruise ship. Much of the decoration which had been painted on her hull was later removed.** *(Clive Harvey)*

The Aquitaine Lounge, as it is now known, has always been one of *Black Prince (ii)*'s most attractive spaces. The clever use of slatted screens tactfully separates the piano bar area from the quieter outer reaches of the room. *(Bruce Peter)*

in addition to the mainly middle-aged aficionados who had so enjoyed those regular voyages to the islands every winter. The 'new' Black Prince (ii) would, it was hoped, attract younger, more active holidaymakers, many of whom might never have cruised before. One aspect of her former self would not change, however – with the age of the mega-cruise ship already dawning, brochures emphasised that she was a smaller, more intimate and more friendly ship than most.

Remodelling an old favourite.

The reconstruction of *Black Prince (ii)* was quite far-reaching and increased her gross tonnage from 9,549 to 11,209. 125 new cabins were built into much of the space which had formerly been occupied by either cars or cargo. Together with the existing cabins, which were thoroughly refurbished, these now enabled the ship to carry up to 527 passengers in accommodation ranging from luxurious suites to small inside cabins. The space which had sometimes acted as a lido and sometimes as a lounge – depending on whether the ship was in cruise or ferry mode – now disappeared but a new two deck-high show lounge was built, fringed with a gallery at the upper level. There were now two pleasantly furnished formal restaurants and, on Sun Deck, an *al fresco* café. Happily, the beautiful forward-facing, wood-panelled lounge was retained, with its slatted screens separating the inner cocktail bar from an outer horse-shoe of quieter space. Decorated, as was much of the ship, with modern art especially selected by the third Fred. Olsen himself, this delightful room has long been recognised as one of the pleasantest spaces to be found on any cruise ship. One of the attractions of *Black Prince (ii)*, especially for older passengers, had always been the convenient layout of her public rooms and this continued to be the case.

To add to the ship's appeal to the active set, a fitness centre was built low down on A Deck and, some years later, a large indoor swimming pool was added – an unusual feature these days. There was now also, of course, an outdoor pool, surrounded by a tiered lido, to accommodate which the ship's stern was built up. But most notably, the aperture in the stern which was a legacy from her days as a ferry, now housed a unique 'Marina Park', which one brochure described as a 'floating leisure centre', adding 'Carried within the body of the ship while she sails, it can be floated out from the stern into calm waters when the ship is at anchor.' From this 60-feet long facility, passengers could enjoy water-skiing, dinghy sailing, scuba-diving and other aquatic sports. The contract with MacGregor-Navire, who designed and constructed this Marina Park, stipulated that they should not produce a similar facility for any other line within a stated period. In fact, so keen were Olsens to ensure that nobody should steal their idea, an early brochure contained a rather fanciful drawing of the ship with the Marina Park extended from the stern but tantalisingly draped so that it was impossible to see exactly what it consisted of.

There were also cosmetic changes to the ship. Design work, including the Prince of Wales' three-feathered emblem and a representation of the Black Prince himself, was painted on the white hull but was considered by some to be rather outlandish. Much of this decoration was eventually removed. On the after deck, two non-functioning sails could be unfurled when the ship was in port – purely for decorative purposes. Perhaps getting carried away with it all, the writer of one of the first brochures claimed: 'That is the clue to the style of the *Black Prince*...... a modern cruise liner that offers today's holiday-maker the leisured shipboard life traditional in the days of sail'.

Black Prince (ii) has three restaurants including the informal conservatory-style Balblom on the top deck. Here we see the stylish Fleur de Lys and Royal Garter. Many British passengers still enjoy dressing for dinner on the several formal nights during each cruise.
(Bruce Peter)

An uneasy start followed by a change of tack.

Now registered in Manila and with a mainly Filipino crew, but still with predominantly Norwegian officers, *Black Prince (ii)* started her new career on the 28th February, 1987, when she sailed from Southampton for Cadiz, Casablanca, the Canary Islands (La Gomera, Santa Cruz de Tenerife and Lanzarote), Madeira, Gibraltar and back to Southampton. It is not unusual for maiden voyages to be troublesome and this one was no exception. In particular, there were passenger complaints, seized on by the press, about inexperienced staff unused to the rigours of a rough crossing of the Bay of Biscay. In due course, the various problems were sorted out and *Black Prince (ii)* quickly regained her good reputation. The master on that first cruise, and many later ones, was Captain Thor Fleten, who, over the years, came to be particularly associated with the ship. A sociable man,

much liked by his passengers, and a very competent seaman who was admired by many of his colleagues, he is often credited with having set the friendly tone which became one of *Black Prince (ii)*'s most endearing characteristics.

The early years of her career as a full-time cruise ship may not have been the success for which Olsens had, no doubt, been hoping. She led a rather unsettled existence, being based variously at Southampton, Tilbury, Venice (with passengers flown out from Britain), the Canaries (also for fly-cruises) and Oslo (for Baltic mini-cruises aimed at the local Norwegian market). There were also problems – a bout of engine trouble, for instance, and a crew strike which left the ship and her passengers stranded at Helsinki. By mid-1990, it seemed that Olsens had withdrawn from the cruise market and they transferred *Black Prince (ii)* to a new ferry service between

The remarkable Marina Park, which is floated out from the stern when *Black Prince (ii)* is at rest in calm waters, offers her more active passengers the opportunity to indulge in water sports. Also to be seen in this picture is the large stern deck lido. *(Postcard, author's collection)*

Gothenburg and Copenhagen. However, the introduction of a Norwegian-owned, Philippine-flagged, largely Filipino-crewed ship into this trade sparked, literally, violent reactions from members of the Swedish and Danish unions and it was reluctantly decided that she would have to be withdrawn.

This unhappy period ended with the transfer of the ship to a hastily-arranged programme of cruises from Southampton to her old haunts in the Canaries and to other southern destinations, starting in September, 1990 and aimed largely at the kind of British passengers who had been so loyal to her and her sister every winter for the twenty years from 1966 onwards. It was a fortunate move – *Black Prince (ii)* quickly regained her old popularity and became one of the most successful ships in the British cruise market. Years later, a well-known cruise guide commented that: 'there are many repeat passengers who wouldn't dream of trying another ship'.

Throughout her career as a full-time cruise ship, she has always spent some time on charter to other operators

and, in particular, to The National Trust for Scotland and to Page & Moy. The National Trust for Scotland have been running cruises since 1953. These were originally annual voyages in small passenger ships which took members round the coast of Scotland in order to visit some of the properties in the Trust's care. In time, larger ships were used for longer voyages to foreign parts. One of these vessels was the British India Line's *Uganda*. In 1984, with *Uganda* now shuttling regularly between Ascension and the Falklands as a troopship, the Trust turned to *Black Prince (ii)*. At that time, the ship had not yet been converted and so she still had her car decks. Passengers who were planning to drive to Leith to join the cruise could therefore be offered the opportunity to garage their cars on board, free of charge.

Limiting the number of passengers to just 400, the Trust found that they had their ideal ship. It was 'a marriage made in Heaven'. Except for two years in the early 1990s, they chartered her annually between 1984 and 2007, latterly for two voyages each year. These were rather different from *Black Prince (ii)*'s usual cruises: the passengers were mainly Scottish; the entertainment was provided by specially recruited Scottish artistes; a piper would usually be playing on the quayside when passengers left or returned to the ship; and a Church of Scotland minister conducted a service every evening which almost always attracted a 'full house'. These were emphatically cultural cruises – Fred. Olsen cruise ships usually have an interesting variety of lecturers on board, but on these National Trust for Scotland voyages the talks, by recognised academics, provided passengers with a quite intensive course of instruction on the culture and history of the places they were about to visit or about the wild-life they would see.

Continuing success.

For some years, when cruising for her owners, *Black Prince (ii)* would sail from Tilbury or Harwich if going northwards to Norway or the Baltic and from Southampton if sailing southwards to the Atlantic Islands or the Mediterranean. Later, many of her summer cruises were switched to Dover, which was being very competitively developed as a cruise port, with the former Dover Harbour railway station now converted into a passenger terminal.

In June, 1994, *Black Prince (ii)* was one of a number of cruise ships which took part in the D. Day celebrations, during which she visited Omaha Beach. Nigel Lingard remembers: 'We carried a shipload of Canadian veterans and the visit included sailing up the Caen Canal twenty miles to the town centre. There the Mayor proudly showed me a warehouse still decorated with a giant Fred. Olsen logo and flag – a leftover from a former cargo service.' The following year, *Black Prince (ii)* made a much lengthier cruise than usual – to the Caribbean – and every winter since then she has made one or two of these longer, more exotic voyages which have taken her to places as distant as Cuba, the Amazon or South Africa. Bearing in mind the purposes for which she was originally designed, she has shewn remarkable adaptability. Inevitably, she has had occasional mishaps – storm damage and, in March 2004, a bout of engine trouble – but she is still the same strong, very safe ship she has always been.

Lately, the addition of other ships to their fleet has prompted Fred. Olsen Cruise Lines to use *Black Prince (ii)* to experiment with new markets, for which her modest size limits the commercial risk. In the early months of 2002, they assigned her to cruises from Cuban ports, with passengers being flown out from Britain. (It was during one of these cruises that she ran aground on a sandbank despite the fact that she had three local pilots on board and was sailing within a marked channel. Her passengers were flown home and after four days she was refloated with relatively little damage.) More happily, she runs cruises from British ports which in recent years have only rarely hosted cruise ships, operating with some success out of Liverpool (with calls to pick up further passengers in Dublin), Greenock, Leith and also Belfast. The construction by the port authorities of a new passenger terminal at Liverpool is a particularly welcome move.

Black Prince (ii) **at Palma de Mallorca in 1999. She has always been a frequent visitor to ports on the various Spanish islands and is said to have called at Santa Cruz de Tenerife more often than any other deep-sea passenger ship.** *(Bruce Peter)*

11.
Black Watch (iii): a World Cruise Ship

As we saw in the previous chapter, *Black Prince (ii)* gradually established herself as one of the most successful ships in the British cruise market. Many passengers who did not relish the idea of trying one of the new generation of large, impersonal vessels, appreciated her relatively modest size and her friendly atmosphere. The combination of British passengers, a largely Filipino crew and mainly Norwegian officers worked extremely well.

From 1987 until 1996, she was a 'singleton' – a one-ship operation. However, in the cruise industry, as in so many others, there are economies of scale. The larger the fleet, the more widely the costs of marketing and administration can be spread and so, provided a cruise line can attract enough passengers to fill an additional ship, the profit per vessel is likely to be increased. By the mid-1990s, Fred Olsen Cruise Lines were looking for another vessel. An additional reason for doing so was the need to maintain their position in a market which was expanding very strongly – the number of British passengers taking a cruise quadrupled between 1990 and 1999 and by 2004 it had topped a million per annum, reaching 1.2 million in 2006.

Persistence rewarded.

The search was not easy but in 1996 Olsens found their ship – one, in fact, which they had been eyeing for some time. She had been completed in June 1972 as the *Royal Viking Star*, the first of three sisters built for the newly formed Royal Viking Line. This concern had been set up by a consortium of three well-known Norwegian shipowners – Det Bergenske Dampskibsselskab (the Bergen Line, whom we have already met in previous chapters), Det Nordenfjeldske Dampskibsselskab and A. F. Klaveness. Each of the partners contributed one vessel, with *Royal Viking Star* being the Bergen Line ship. Her naming ceremony was performed by Mrs. Thor Heyerdahl, the wife of the Norwegian anthropologist of *Kon-Tiki* fame. (In view of the fact that the ship later passed into Olsen hands, this was a happy coincidence since Thor Heyerdahl and the third Fred. Olsen were long-standing friends and, indeed, they co-operated in projects related to the study of pyramid-building cultures and their spread westwards from the Middle East.)

Designed by Tage Wandborg and built in Finland at the Helsinki yard of the Wärtsilä company, the *Royal Viking Star* and her two sisters had a distinctive profile

A striking aerial view of the *Royal Viking Star* before her lengthening in 1981. For some years, the Royal Viking Line ships were among the most prestigious vessels in the cruise market, taking wealthy, mainly American passengers on worldwide itineraries. *(Author's collection)*

The former *Royal Viking Star*, by now sailing as Norwegian Cruise Line's *Westward*, is here seen at Puerto Vallarta, Mexico in April, 1992. She proved, however, to be sadly ill-suited to NCL's mass-market operation. (*Timothy J. Dacey*)

with a flared and very raked bow and a slender funnel which was flanked by windscoops and was obviously inspired by that of the recently completed *QE2*. They were amongst the most notable cruise ships of the day, consistently being awarded the highest ranking by the cruise guides. Furnished in a modern, rather spare but very comfortable style, they gained a fine reputation for good service and for the wide-ranging itineraries, including World cruises, which they offered to their mainly American clientele. They were, in fact, 'top of the market' ships and their cruises were priced accordingly. Although at first the Royal Viking Line struggled to make a profit, it gradually established itself as a leader in the cruise business.

As built, the 21,847 gross tons *Royal Viking Star* was a particularly roomy ship carrying no more than 539 passengers, a number which proved to be barely economic. The Bergen Line directors in particular were keen to have the three sisters lengthened in order to increase their passenger capacity. (This is said to have been one of the reasons why discussions regarding a possible merger of Royal Viking with the Norwegian America Line fell through. Norwegian America maintained that increasing the passenger numbers would

make the ships less exclusive and therefore less attractive to their well-heeled clients who relished their 'club-like' atmosphere.) In 1981, the *Royal Viking Star* was sent to Bremerhaven for the lengthening to take place. She was sliced in two slightly aft of the bridge and a new 27.7 metre mid-section, built by AG Weser Seebeckwerft, was inserted. As a result, her passenger capacity was increased from 539 to 758 and her gross tonnage rose to 28,221. She remained a fine cruise ship with, for instance, a very high proportion of cabins having either windows or portholes. Unfortunately, however, the Norwegian America Line's contention tha she, and her sisters which were similarly lengthened, would lose some of their exclusive appeal proved to be correct. Furthermore, competition at the top end of the market was increasing, with some former Royal Viking passengers now transferring their allegiance to newer ships such as the smaller and even more exclusive 110-passenger cruising yachts of Sea Goddess Cruises.

A. F. Klaveness had withdrawn from the Royal Viking consortium in 1977 and in 1984 the remaining partners sold the line and its ships to the Kloster Cruise group of Oslo. Klosters were the owners of the Norwegian Caribbean Line (later the Norwegian Cruise Line), one of

Black Watch (iii) **(ex-*Royal Viking Star*) moored at Greenwich. Since her purchase and complete refurbishment by Fred. Olsen Cruise Lines, she has regained much of her old appeal and is once more noted for her Round the World cruises and other lengthy voyages to far-flung ports.** *(Clive Harvey)*

the pioneers of the modern, Florida-based, mass-market cruise industry. Unfortunately, there were soon reports that standards on the newly-acquired Royal Viking ships were beginning to slip. In 1990, the *Royal Viking Star* was transferred within the Kloster group to the Norwegian Cruise Line, who renamed her *Westward* and used her for 7-day cruises to Bermuda and to the Mexican Riviera amongst other destinations. But she was a misfit, too grand for their 'fun ship' concept of cruising. Timothy Dacey, who had known her as the *Royal Viking Star*, was dismayed to find that 'a large portion of the dining room had been removed to create a fun room ..... and her elegant public rooms looked tatty when lined with slot machines'. Furthermore, despite the 1981 lengthening, she still carried fewer passengers than the mass-market Norwegian Cruise Line needed in a ship of this size. It was something of a relief when, in 1994, she was transferred to another company within the Kloster group, the rather more up-market, Greek-managed Royal Cruise Line, and became their *Star Odyssey*, mainly operating out of New York and Vancouver.

Opportunity seized.

However, Klosters were by now labouring under a heavy weight of debt as they struggled to compete with better capitalised rivals. In 1996, they suddenly closed down the Royal Cruise Line and offered the *Star Odyssey*

for sale. Olsens saw their opportunity, buying her through a third party and being reported to have paid $55million for her. They took delivery in Piraeus in early October, 1996 and then spent a further £4 million on having her refurbished by A & P Southampton. Now called *Black Watch (iii)*, she was well-suited to her new owners' purposes – larger than *Black Prince (ii)*, but not overwhelmingly so, and designed to be able to undertake longer cruises.

The interior décor was re-worked by the London firm of McNeece, who restored some dignity to the ship and gave her a typical Fred. Olsen ambience. Tartan carpeting was laid in what was now called the Braemar Lounge and throughout the public rooms there were some striking modern artworks, together with models, bow decorations and photographs commemorating previous Olsen ships. The photographs were accompanied by informative captions written by the third Fred. Olsen himself. Some of the spacious feeling for which the ship had once been noted was regained and, while she still had plenty of facilities for livelier enjoyment, there were some pleasant quiet areas. One of the author's favourites is The Observatory, a horse shoe-shaped lounge and bar situated above the bridge. It is a civilised sanctuary in which to relax and gaze out over the sea. Another feature which is much appreciated is the broad open promenade which completely encircles the ship at Lido Deck level.

The spacious and comfortable Braemar Lounge on *Black Watch (iii)*, where afternoon tea is served and where a pianist plays before dinner, is notable for its coffered ceiling and for the striking array of artworks on its walls. *(Bruce Peter)*

Another civilised lounge and bar on *Black Watch (iii)* is The Observatory, situated above the bridge. Here passengers can enjoy splendid views over the sea while sipping their aperitifs. Binoculars are provided. *(Bruce Peter)*

The Dalreoch Room is a pleasant lounge for those who wish to read, play games — or simply relax. Elsewhere, ***Black Watch (iii)*** **offers her passengers a variety of entertainments and has very ample open air facilities.** *(Bruce Peter)*

Following her refurbishment, *Black Watch (iii)*'s standard passenger capacity became 761 with a maximum occupancy of 843. One result of her 'Olsenisation' was that a number of cabins were converted to single occupancy.

The introduction of a second ship was a major step for Fred. Olsen Cruise Lines since they now had about 150 per cent more berths to fill. Unfortunately, *Black Watch (iii)* did not get off to a good start. Her arrival at Dover on the 12th November, 1996 to be introduced to the press and the travel trade was embarrassingly delayed by several hours owing to engine problems. Her first cruise was a three-week trip to the eastern Mediterranean but the second, a 64-night Round Africa voyage, had to be cut short because of a recurrence of trouble in two of her four 9-cylinder Sulzer diesel engines while she was off the coast of Turkey. She limped to Malta for repairs and most of her passengers were flown back to Britain, with those who

In 2005, *Black Watch (iii)* was given a far-reaching refit which, amongst much else, included the replacement of her main engines. Here we see one of the original units being removed through an aperture cut in the side of her hull. *(Fred. Olsen & Co.)*

were averse to air travel being returned by ferry and coach. In those early days, trouble was also encountered with the plumbing system. However, these problems were rectified and after her nearly disastrous start – which, it was rumoured, may have been partly attributable to skimped maintenance by some of her previous crews – *Black Watch (iii)* soon began to acquire a reputation as a thoroughly pleasant and comfortable vessel. She is, for instance, 'a good sea boat', well able to cope with rough conditions.

She makes many two- and three-week cruises, usually from either Dover or Southampton, but it is for her lengthier voyages that she has become particularly noted. Early examples included one in September, 1997 which took her across the Atlantic to visit four Canadian ports and five in the United States, including New York. Then, a few months later, she made an 82-night Far Eastern cruise. Other Oriental cruises followed in later years, and several voyages round South America. In January, 2004, she rejoined the select ranks of ships which make Round the World Cruises when she set off from Southampton on a voyage whose many calls included a notable visit to Sydney. She was once again running on the kind of itineraries for which, with her ample storage capacity for fuel, water and provisions and her spacious rooms, she had originally been designed.

A new heart for an old favourite.

After some years, elaborate plans were laid for a major investment which would extend her life since it was considered that it was no longer economic to build a completely new 30,000-ton ship to carry a mere 800 passengers. In mid-April, 2005 *Black Watch (iii)*, newly returned from another World Cruise, went to the Blohm & Voss yard at Hamburg for a refit lasting two months. This involved the replacement of her old Sulzer engines by four new MAN/B&W 7-cylinder units. These are a good 2 knots faster and much less thirsty than the old ones and must have proved an even better investment than anticipated, given the huge rise in oil prices which has since taken place. They also emit much less exhaust. In addition, new gearing and new generators were installed. The old machinery was removed, and the replacement units were inserted, through large apertures which had been cut in the ship's sides as she lay in dry dock. New and more efficient propellers were also fitted and, during a general refurbishment of the passenger quarters, fourteen new balcony suites were created and more cabins on Bridge Deck were given balconies, bringing the total with this facility to 67. It was expected that, with her still sound hull, generally spacious cabins and tasteful public rooms, *Black Watch (iii)* would be able to compete in the cruise market for at least another ten years but would retain all her old charm and character. On her return to service in June, 2005 she resumed her previous varied schedule, which includes short 4-day 'taster' cruises, partly intended to introduce newcomers to the joys of cruising; 1-, 2- and 3-week voyages to the usual European destinations; and, of course, long and prestigious voyages to more distant and exotic parts.

The success of the refit did not go un-noticed by the operators of her former sister ship *Royal Viking Sea*, now sailing as the *Albatros*, and some time afterwards they sent her to Blohm & Voss for a similar transformation, albeit with engines of a different type. Furthermore, Olsens themselves bought the other sister, the former *Royal Viking Sky*, and gave her the same treatment as *Black Watch (iii)* – but that is another story which must await Chapter Thirteen.

A stern view of *Black Watch (iii)* as she rests at anchor off Portoferraio one day in July, 1997, awaiting the return of passengers who have gone ashore on excursions. Note the size of her after deck. *(Clive Harvey)*

12.
The Streamlined *Braemar (iii)*

By the start of the new Millennium, the success of *Black Watch (iii)* and the continuing popularity of *Black Prince (ii)* were prompting Fred. Olsen Cruise Lines to seek a third vessel. Again, the search was not easy. Very few new cruise ships of the moderate size which Olsens and their passengers preferred had been built in recent years. Most lines were opting for the 'benefits of scale' and were introducing ever larger ships which carried ever bigger complements of passengers. Olsens, though, knew from experience that there was still a market in Britain for comfortable vessels of medium size which could offer a more personal 'cruise experience' and could enter ports too restricted for the new giants. Since it had arguably become uneconomic to build new ships of this scale, they would have to scour the second-hand market.

At last, in early 2001 following the bankruptcy of the Commodore Cruise Line, the opportunity arose to acquire a good vessel which was to their taste. Although she had so far had a somewhat chequered career, the 19,089 gross tons *Crown Dynasty* was a handy-sized and very modern ship with accommodation for up to 916 passengers. (In fact, the changes made by Olsens before she entered their service, including making a number of cabins available for single occupancy, reduced this figure to 727 in lower berths, with a maximum of 819.)

She was one of a pair which had been ordered from the Union Naval de Levante shipyard in Valencia for the Crown Cruise Line, managed by yet another Norwegian shipowner, Mr. Oddmund Grunstad. Delivered in 1993 and named by Mrs. Betty Ford, the wife of the former President of the United States, the *Crown Dynasty* was employed in the Caribbean market. However, financial difficulties soon led to the Crown Cruise Line operation being taken over by the Commodore Cruise Line. Briefly, under a joint marketing arrangement with Cunard, the *Crown Dynasty* was renamed *Cunard Dynasty*. Then, in 1997-98 she became successively *Crown Majesty* for a short charter to the Majesty Cruise Line and *Norwegian Dynasty* while under charter to the Norwegian Cruise Line, who based her on the West Coast of America. Eventually, she returned to Commodore, or more precisely to their Crown Cruise Line subsidiary, and resumed the name of *Crown Dynasty*. For a time, she was employed on the Bermuda run from Philadelphia and from Baltimore.

Sleek, light and airy.

Following her purchase by Olsens, she was sent to the Blohm & Voss shipyard at Hamburg to be thoroughly refurbished. The work, which was said to have cost $10 million, also included enlarging her water and fuel tanks. This was necessary because she had been specifically designed for 7-day cruises in the Caribbean. A modern-looking ship with a sleek and strikingly streamlined profile, she has a spacious but well-sheltered top deck lido and an encircling open promenade lower down. As had become customary with passenger ships of her generation, the lifeboats are stowed inboard above one of the lower decks. Internally, her most notable feature is a five deck-high atrium, glass-walled on one side to give a spectacular view of the sea. Olsens retained her original layout, which had been designed by the noted firm of Yran & Storbraaten, but they had the décor re-styled to create a light and airy atmosphere, well-suited to cruising in the tropics. Even such a demanding observer as Clive Harvey, the editor of *Sea Lines*, admitted to being charmed by the result. The restaurant, for instance – situated at the stern and with

The Spanish-built *Crown Dynasty* in the colours of the now defunct Crown Cruise Line. When she was delivered in 1993, the age of the mega-ship was already underway and it was unusual for a cruise company to be taking delivery of a medium-sized ship of this kind.
(Author's collection)

Braemar (iii) displays her ultra-modern lines. The purchase of the former *Crown Dynasty* in 2001 enabled Fred. Olsen to extend their range of cruises, particularly adding Caribbean fly-cruises in the winter months. *(Fred.Olsen & Co., author's collection)*

some of the outer tables having fine sea views – now had a cool and tasteful colour scheme of cream and fawn and the Neptune Lounge was furnished in lemon and terra cotta. There were still the traditional Olsen touches, however – tartan carpeting in some rooms and artworks from the 1953 *Braemar (i)*, together with an attractive model of that ship.

Four 8-cylinder 4-stroke diesel engines, of Wärtsilä design but built in Spain, give her a service speed of 18½ knots with more in reserve. As we have seen, she had been a purpose-built ship, specially designed to meet the requirements of her original owners. As a result, her relatively shallow draught enabled her to enter many smaller ports denied to deeper vessels. And although Olsens had her storage capacity increased after they purchased her, she was still limited to a range of 16 or 17 days. Given the type of cruises for which they intended to use her, however, this was not a handicap. She now had a traditional Olsen name, *Braemar (iii)*.

A new fly-cruise programme.

Just as the purchase of *Black Watch (iii)* enabled Olsens to enter the long distance cruise market, so the advent of the *Braemar (iii)* gave them the opportunity of adding fly-cruises to their programme. Hitherto, they had concentrated mainly on voyages starting and finishing in British ports, a policy popular with passengers who did not enjoy long flights and who appreciated being able to take more luggage than would have been feasible on a fly-cruise. However, there is a considerable market for Caribbean cruises among people who do not mind flying and who wish to get away from the unpredictable British winters. The acquisition of *Braemar (iii)* enabled Olsens to tap into this. She started her new career nearer to home, however, with a Scandinavian cruise which left Dover on the 11th August, 2001. Very appropriately, during a call at Dundee on her way north, she offered her passengers an excursion to the Highland village after which she had been named.

After that, a regular pattern developed: Caribbean or Amazon voyages, often starting from Bridgetown, Barbados, in the Winter; Baltic and Norwegian cruises in the summer months; Mediterranean and Atlantic islands cruises in the 'shoulder seasons'. Positioning voyages taking the ship across the Atlantic, to and from the Caribbean, were also offered at the beginning and end of each winter season. In November, 2002, as she reached the end of a passage which took her 800 miles up the Amazon, *Braemar (iii)* inaugurated the new cruise terminal at Manaos.

As we saw in Chapter Ten, Olsens have lately been developing the British regional market for cruises, mainly with *Black Prince (ii)*. By 2006, increasing demand meant that *Black Prince (ii)* became almost exclusively the line's west coast ship, while *Braemar (iii)* began some summer sailings from Leith and Newcastle. Thus the Fred. Olsen flag was again seen at Tyne Commission Quay where it was once such a familiar sight.

Unusually for a ship of her size, *Braemar (iii)* has a spectacular five deck-high atrium. Like many of the spaces onboard, it is particularly airy. For this reason, and because of her large top deck lido, *Braemar (iii)* is particularly suited to Caribbean cruising. *(Bruce Peter)*

Lengthening but not overwhelming.

The Olsens have a record of willingness to modify their ships, sometimes very innovatively. Some years ago, they were rumoured to have commissioned a series of test tank experiments with a model of *Braemar (iii)*'s hull in order to ascertain whether it would be advantageous to make any changes. At the time, nothing was done but in June, 2007 it was announced that, following the lengthening of the *Balmoral* (see Chapter Fourteen), *Braemar* too would go to Blohm & Voss in Hamburg for a similar operation. In May – June 2008, a new 31.2 metre midsection would be inserted in the hull and Deck 8 would be extended both fore and aft. The new forward end of this deck would house an Observatory Lounge, thus replicating this very pleasant feature on *Black Watch (iii)* and *Boudicca*. There would also be an additional restaurant and, as on

Balmoral, a bar 'designed on the concept of a British pub'. Another innovation would be a dedicated arts and crafts room. Outside, on the enlarged upper deck, there would now be a bigger lido area and a second swimming pool. In addition, it would be possible to increase the amount of premium accommodation, so that there would now be more cabins and suites with balconies. In all, there would be 250 extra lower berths bringing the total up to 977. Although *Braemar (iii)* would now be a somewhat larger ship, she would still carry a comfortably modest number of passengers and the aim would be to ensure that there was little change to the atmosphere on board. One advantage of the added length of hull would be that her sea-keeping qualities would be improved.

The changes made to *Braemar (iii)* and the introduction of the *Balmoral* will enable Fred. Olsen

The Palms Café on *Braemar (iii)* has a light, tropical feeling. While certainly not lacking in style, it represents a pleasantly relaxed 'dining alternative' to the very elegant but more formal main restaurant. *(Bruce Peter)*

With local river boats in the foreground, *Braemar (iii)* is moored at Paratins on the Amazon on the 30th November, 2002. Cruises up the Amazon have become a regular feature of her annual schedule. *(Clive Harvey)*

Cruise Lines to extend their range of itineraries. The Summer of 2008 will see *Braemar (iii)* based in Civitavecchia (the port for Rome) for a programme of Mediterranean cruises, with her predominantly British passengers being flown out to join her. In Winter, 2008-09 she will be stationed in Miami, from where she will make Caribbean cruises. While it is hoped that a certain number of Americans will be attracted to these voyages, it is intended that the ship will still carry mainly British passengers and that the atmosphere will remain very British. Olsens will emphatically not be competing for the mass-market trade and it is indicative of this that all slot machines have now been removed from their ships. *Braemar (iii)*'s place as the line's 'east coast ship' operating out of Leith and Newcastle in the summer months and her usual schedule of winter cruises out of Georgetown, Barbados will both be taken over by *Boudicca*.

Olsens do not forget their history and the décor on *Braemar (iii)* includes artworks from the first *Braemar*, such as this attractive wooden plaque. Also on display is a fine model of that notable ship. *(Author)*

13.
Boudicca, the Stylish

2005 was a significant year for Fred. Olsen Cruise Lines. Not only did they send *Black Watch (iii)* to be re-engined and upgraded but, almost simultaneously, they surprised the cruise world by announcing the purchase of one of her sisters. This was the former *Royal Viking Sky*, the second of the three notable ships which had established the Royal Viking Line as one of the most prestigious (and envied) companies in the 1970s cruise industry (see Chapter Eleven).

The *Royal Viking Sky* was built, like her two sisters, by OY Wärtsilä at their Helsinki yard. On completion in June, 1973 she was handed over to her new owners, Det Nordenfjeldske Dampskibsselskab of Trondheim, one of the three partners in the new line, each of whom contributed a single ship. Apart from some minor variations in her interior arrangements and a sometimes different décor, the *Royal Viking Sky* was virtually identical to the first of the trio, the *Royal Viking Star* (i.e.: the future *Black Watch (iii)*). The very successful basic design of

these ships was the work of Tage Wandborg of the Copenhagen firm of Knud E. Hansen A/S, while the rather modernistic interiors came from the drawing board of the Oslo-based Finn Nilsson. As it happened, Nilsson had worked with Arnstein Arneberg on the passenger areas of Fred. Olsen's outstanding mini-liners *Blenheim (ii)* and *Braemar (i)* in the early 1950s (see Chapter Six).

As built, the Royal Viking trio were particularly roomy ships, each of which carried a maximum of little more than 550 passengers in her spacious public rooms and accommodation. However, in 1982, the *Royal Viking Sky*, like her sisters, underwent a difficult operation in which the entire ship was severed transversely, dividing her into two separate parts. A new mid-section was then inserted between them and the three parts were joined together. When she left the AG Weser Seebeckwerft yard at Bremerhaven in the November, she had been lengthened by 91 feet and could now house up to 752 passengers. Her gross tonnage had risen from 21,891 to 28,078.

Her lights reflecting in the harbour waters, *Boudicca* makes a fine sight as dusk falls over Havana during a visit she made to the Cuban capital in 2007. *(Bruce Peter)*

Since her early days as *Royal Viking Sky*, *Boudicca* has had a very varied career, passing through many hands. Here we see her as *Superstar Capricorn* at Singapore, with a bunkering barge alongside. *Boudicca* is, of course, a sister to *Black Watch (iii)*. *(Jonathan Boonzaier)*

Several new careers.

A minor distinction for the *Royal Viking Sky* was that she was one of the ships, although by no means the main one, used as a setting for on-board scenes in the hugely popular, long-running American television series *The Love Boat*.

In 1984, the Royal Viking Line was acquired by the Kloster group of Oslo. By now, the three sisters were beginning to lose some of the very special appeal they had once had as some of the best-run and most exclusive ships in the worldwide luxury cruise market. Before long, they were being dispersed. The *Royal Viking Sky* was transferred in 1991 to Kloster's own Norwegian Caribbean Line subsidiary, becoming their *Sunward*. Like her sister *Westward* (the former *Royal Viking Star*), she proved ill at ease in her new career, particularly when she was running 3- and 4-day 'fun cruises' from Miami to the Bahamas. She also appeared on the European side of the Atlantic, making Baltic cruises. To enable her to cater for her new, perhaps livelier and certainly much less formal passengers, a children's playroom, a video arcade and a large casino had been installed.

Her sale in 1992 to the Birka Line of Mariehamn in the Finnish Åland Islands marked the beginning of a somewhat peripatetic period in which she frequently passed from one line to another and had only intermittent success. Birka Line, who called their new acquisition *Birka Queen*, specialise in brief cruises from Stockholm to Mariehamn and back, offering Swedish passengers the opportunity for duty-free shopping and general merrymaking. Very soon, however, Birka chartered her back for a few months to Norwegian Caribbean, now known as Norwegian Cruise Line, and then to Princess Cruises. Now under the name *Golden Princess* and after a major refurbishment, she went out to the West Coast of America, where Princess based her in San Francisco and in Los Angeles and used her for cruises to Alaska in the Summer and southwards to Mexican ports in the Winter. Her excellent cabin accommodation could now be put to better use than of late.

In 1996, at the end of the three-year charter to Princess, Birka sold her to Star Cruises, belonging to the Genting group. Genting, based in Malaysia and owners of hotels and resorts, were investing large sums in building up a fleet of ships to develop the Asian cruise market. After giving her another refit, this time to adapt her to Asian tastes, Star Cruises used the ship mainly for short cruises out of Keelung in Taiwan to the famous island of Okinawa and other Japanese destinations under the name *Superstar Capricorn*. There was, though, a brief and unsuccessful interlude in Spring, 1998 when she was based in New York for overnight gambling cruises. When I saw her during that period, she was looking distinctly run down.

The downward spiral continued when she moved on once more, this time being chartered to the South Korean concern Hyundai Merchant Marine Co. They called her *Hyundai Kumgang* and placed her in a regular cruise service carrying pilgrims and tourists to the Kumgang Mountains region of North Korea. This was a ground-breaking move, given the history of relations between North and South Korea, and the inaugural sailing in November, 1998 was watched by a large crowd and celebrated with a spectacular fireworks display. However, there were constant disputes between Hyundai and the North Korean authorities and wintertime passenger bookings were not encouraged by the rough weather often encountered in the area. Eventually, after heavy losses, Hyundai withdrew from the cruise business and the *Hyundai Kumgang* lay idle. When the charter expired in November, 2001, Hyundai returned her to Star Cruises, who once again called her *Superstar Capricorn*. She was said to be in need of considerable refurbishment.

Although Star used her for a while for cruises out of Bangkok, the future was by now looking bleak for this once-famous ship. However, by 2004 there was renewed interest in her. Indeed, there were strong rumours that she might go to Fred. Olsen Cruise Lines, who were having great success with her sister ship, now *Black Watch (iii)*, and were known to be keen to add a fourth vessel to their fleet. In the event, she was bought by associates of the Spanish travel company Iberojet who renamed her *Grand Latino* for cruises out of Barcelona.

Despite the fact that the Spaniards spent heavily on restoring her, she did not remain with them for long. In January, 2005 it was announced that she was being sold to Olsens. At first, they made it known that they would call her *Boadicea*. This was a new name for an Olsen ship but commemorated the great English first century heroine, queen of the Icenae tribe, who, in a chariot with flailing sword blades fixed to its wheels, led her followers to victory in several battles against the usually all-conquering Romans before she was herself defeated and committed suicide. The name was a very apt choice for a ship aimed primarily at the British market – Britons of a certain cruising generation were likely to recall the story of Boadicea from their school-days and might well feel that the country has often been at its greatest when led by a formidable woman. A few weeks after the announcement, however, there was another. The name would now become *Boudicca* – the same lady but a different spelling, less familiar to the general public but currently favoured by the academics.

One of the more exotic episodes in *Boudicca*'s previous career was her stint as *Hyundai Kumgang*, running cruises from South Korea to the Kumgang Mountains region of North Korea. Here is a brochure advertising them. (*Jonathan Boonzaier collection*)

A great lady restored.

Olsens took delivery of the ship at Valencia at the end of October, 2005 and sailed her to Santa Cruz de Tenerife, where, alongside the passenger quay, some of their own employees performed such initial tasks as gutting many of the public rooms, stripping decks, etc. This was in preparation for a far-reaching refit which was to take place at the Blohm & Voss yard in Hamburg. In fact, the *Boudicca* was to undergo a similar transformation to the one which was proving so successful with *Black Watch (iii)* – four new MAN/B&W engines, new gearboxes, new generators, new propellers, new balcony suites and balconies added to some other cabins.

There was to be more, however. Her public rooms were to be largely re-modelled and furnished in a slightly more modern style than those on her sister. The interior design was the work of the London firm of SPACE: The Design Practice, which had sprung from McNeece who had previously worked for Olsens. The third Fred. Olsen's daughter Merete was also very much involved in the process and, as usual, the many artworks were selected by Mr. Olsen himself. From all this, there has emerged a very elegant ship, well able to regain much of the regard in which she was held in her distinguished early years.

현 대 상 선 주 식 회 사
금 강 개 발 산 업 주 식 회 사

After buying *Superstar Capricorn* in 2005, Olsens spent heavily on re-engining and refitting her. By the time she emerged as *Boudicca*, her public rooms had been almost completely refurnished and were decorated with a huge number of artworks. This quiet corner of a lounge is typical. *(Author)*

Particularly pleasing is The Secret Garden, a buffet restaurant which has much more style than the glorified motorway service station cafés which are the equivalent rooms on so many other ships. The construction of this room and the various changes which had been made to the ship during the different stages of her complicated career have given her public spaces a slightly more divided feel than those on *Black Watch (iii)*, but they all have a very fresh and attractive atmosphere. The work at Blohm & Voss lasted from early December, 2005 until mid-February, 2006.

Boudicca's first cruise started at Dover on the 25th February, 2006 and, very fittingly for an Olsen ship, took her to the Canary Islands. She has since established herself as a popular member of the fleet, running a varied programme of cruises of different lengths. One of her first longer voyages was her Christmas and New Year cruise, 2006-7 which took her out to the Caribbean and back. In Summer 2008, following the lengthening of *Braemar (iii)*, *Boudicca* will take over from that ship her regular programme of cruises out of Leith and Newcastle and, in the following Winter, the season of Caribbean cruises out of Bridgetown, Barbados.

14.
Balmoral, the new flagship

Very soon after *Boudicca*'s entry into service, rumours began to circulate that Olsens were looking for a further addition to their growing cruise fleet. Then in May, 2006 they announced that, through a Singapore-based subsidiary, they would be purchasing the very modern 34,232 gross tons *Norwegian Crown*. The transaction actually took place in August but the ship was immediately chartered back to her former owners, Norwegian Cruise Line, with the intention that she would continue to sail for them until November, 2007. Olsens would then gain full possession of her and would call her *Balmoral*. In naming their biggest cruise ship after the Scottish home of the British monarch, the company has emphasised yet again its strong British connections.

A further announcement, made in April 2007, sprang the surprise news that before entering service the *Balmoral* would be lengthened by the insertion of a new 30.4 metre (99 ft. 8ins) mid-section. Interestingly, her original design had made provision for a possible lengthening at a later date. As the *Norwegian Crown* she had accommodated up to 1,209 passengers but after the lengthening this number would become 1,340. Nevertheless, there has been no question of cramming in as many passengers as possible and, although she can carry a larger number than the other ships of the fleet, the aim is still to provide the kind of comfortable, uncongested cruise experience for which Olsens have become noted. Compared with the new generation of 180,000 or 200,000-tonners being introduced elsewhere, which carry well over 3,000 passengers, *Balmoral* is still a very manageably-sized vessel. The much-appreciated Fred. Olsen policy of providing a number of cabins for single passengers has been maintained and, indeed, with 78 such cabins, *Balmoral* now has the second largest number of any current cruise ship. (Most, these days, do not have any.) There are also nine cabins for disabled passengers. In addition, as a result of the conversion the number of cabins and suites with balconies has been increased to 119.

The ship was built in 1987-88 as the *Crown Odyssey* at the German port of Papenburg by Jos. L Meyer, a firm renowned for the quality of its work. Ordered for the Greek-managed but American-financed Royal Cruise Line, she was yet another product of the busy design office of the firm of Knud E. Hansen in Copenhagen, where she was the work of Holger Terpet. He gave her a very distinctive streamlined profile, with a substantial but shapely funnel and a large, round top deck observation lounge. (When she was introduced, one enthusiastic writer described the *Crown Odyssey* as 'the world's most window-full ship'.) Her interiors were in the glossy style

***Crown Odyssey* was built for the Royal Cruise Line, another once-famous company which has since disappeared. Here she is seen at Tilbury on the 5th June, 1988 during her delivery voyage from her German builders.** *(Clive Harvey)*

then fashionable among cruise ships, with acres of marble, stainless steel, chrome and glass and hundreds of bright lights. To some tastes she was smart and sophisticated; to others she seemed glitzy. There was no doubt, though, that she was a very fine ship.

Whatever one's view of the aesthetics of the *Crown Odyssey*'s interiors, there could be no denying that technically she was very advanced. In particular, she was an early example – it is sometimes claimed, the first – of a vessel powered by a 'father and son' propulsion system. One of the problems with marine diesel engines is that they are much more efficient and smooth-running at some speeds than at others. In addition, operating them slowly for long periods can subject them to damaging strains. The 'father and son' system provides a solution to these problems. Put simply, each propeller is driven by a dual unit of one powerful engine and one less powerful. With each engine consistently running at its most efficient speed, there are three options: slow (the lower-rated engine operating on its own); medium (the more powerful engine operating on its own); or fast (both engines running in tandem). If, as in the case of the *Crown Odyssey*, power is transmitted to the propellers via two-speed gearing, the number of efficient options is doubled. Her engines were built by the Krupp MaK Maschinenbau of Kiel, the two 'fathers' having eight cylinders each and the two 'sons' having six.

Most of Royal Cruise Line's passengers were American, particularly from the West Coast. The crew was Greek and *Crown Odyssey* offered a variety of rather select cruises in various parts of the World. However, in the mid- and late-1980s, a 'Big Bang' was taking place in the cruise business and several of the smaller firms were absorbed by the emerging giants. In 1990, only two years after taking delivery of the new ship, the Royal Cruise Line was bought by the Kloster group. Under this new ownership, it continued much as before for a while but in early 1996 it was quite suddenly closed down and the *Crown Odyssey* was transferred to the group's main constituent, the Norwegian Cruise Line. They renamed her *Norwegian Crown* and used her in a variety of cruising areas – Alaska, the Caribbean, Europe, South America and on the Bermuda run.

After four years with Norwegian Cruise Line, her career changed direction again when she was transferred, still within the Kloster group, to the Orient Lines. This was not the old Orient Line, once famous for its passenger and mail service between Britain and Australia, and also as one of the pioneers of the cruise business. That company had disappeared in the 1960s during a reorganisation of the parent P&O group's Australian services. The distinguished Orient name had, however, been revived by the serial shipping entrepreneur Gerry Herrod when he set up a new cruise company in the early 1990s using a former Russian liner which he renamed *Marco Polo*. As had become his wont, once his company was well-established, he sold it – in this case to Klosters. In early 2000, with Orient Lines seeming to need a second ship, the *Norwegian Crown* was given a refit at the Sembawang yard in Singapore and brought in to join the *Marco Polo*. Once again bearing her original name of *Crown Odyssey*, she now had a dark blue hull, which is unusual for a cruise ship these days. She divided her time between the Mediterranean and so-called exploration cruises to more exotic destinations, often in the Middle East and the East. However, in 2003, with the political situation deterring

By 2003, *Crown Odyssey* had become *Norwegian Crown*, as we see her here in Singapore following a refit which included building additional superstructure over the bridge. Temporarily, she is wearing the funnel colours of Orient Lines, her previous operators. (*Jonathan Boonzaier*)

Following her purchase by Olsens, she has been lengthened and her interiors have been transformed. Now called *Balmoral*, she has become an extremely elegant vessel. She is notable for the number of windows and portholes which illuminate her interiors. *(Fred. Olsen Cruise Lines)*

many passengers from venturing to these areas, she was returned to the Norwegian Cruise Line who had additional superstructure built over her bridge and gave her back her old name of *Norwegian Crown*. This almost constant churning has now, it would seem, come to an end and she has found a home with Fred. Olsen Cruise Lines.

The new mid-section has been constructed at Bremerhaven and some of the initial stripping of the old interiors has taken place while the ship has been crossing the Atlantic after being handed over by the Norwegian Caribbean Line. The insertion of the mid-section and the rest of the conversion work has then taken place at the Blohm & Voss yard in Hamburg. Not only has the greater length given scope for increasing the number of cabins and suites but it has also made space for a bigger sun deck area and an extra swimming pool, not to mention two additional small restaurants and a further bar. Passengers familiar with *Black Watch* and *Boudicca* will be pleased to know that *Balmoral*, too, has a pleasant observation lounge. She is, in fact, an extremely well-equipped ship. As with the *Boudicca*, the transformation of the interiors has been handled by SPACE: The Design Practice, with the project being led by Mark Hilferty. The result is in restful contrast to the ship's original 1980s gloss and glitz.

Balmoral is due to depart from Dover on her Inaugural

Cruise on the 30th January, 2008. It will take her on a traditional Olsen itinerary to Spain, Portugal, the Canaries and Madeira. Later, she will cross to Miami for cruises to the Caribbean and Central America before returning to Europe for a short Mediterranean programme based on the Italian ports of Civitavecchia and Venice. After further cruises from Dover, including one to the Maritime coast of Canada and to New York, she will make her first World Cruise for Olsens. This will be one of two in the company's programme during the Winter of 2008-9 – the other, of course, will be made by *Black Watch (iii)*, which will be circumnavigating in a westabout direction via the Caribbean, the Panama Canal, the South Pacific, Australia and the Cape of Good Hope. *Balmoral*, on the other hand, will be going eastabout and on a more northerly course. This will take her through the Mediterranean, the Suez Canal and the Red Sea, then to India, Singapore, Vietnam, several ports in China before going on to South Korea, Japan, the far east of Russia, Alaska and down the West Coast of Canada, America, Mexico and Guatemala before passing through the Panama Canal, then homeward via the Caribbean and the Azores – truly a remarkable voyage.

Fleet List

Notes: b.p. = length between perpendiculars. o.a. = length overall.

Where a ship has had other owners besides Olsens, the town or city which follows the owners' name is the location of their headquarters rather than the ship's port of registry.

Færder (1901 – 1916)
Completed 1882 by W. Doxford & Sons, Sunderland as *Celynen* for T. Beynon, Newport. 1,484 gross tons. 250 ft. 0ins b.p. x 36 ft. 1in. Iron Hull. 2-cylinder compound steam engine by W. Doxford & Sons, 160 NHP. Single screw. Bought by Pile & Co., 1899. Bought by Dampskibsselskab Færder, Christiania and renamed *Færder*, 1899. Taken over by Fred. Olsen, 1901. Sold to A/S Frogner (Alexander Bech), Christiania and renamed *Spro*, 1916. Torpedoed, 1917.

Scotland (i) (1901 – 1903)
Completed 1889 by Grangemouth Dockyard Co., Grangemouth for Dampskibsselskab Færder, Christiania. 841 gross tons. 187 ft. 7ins b.p. x 29 ft. 1in. 3-cylinder triple-expansion steam engine by Hawthorns & Co., Leith . 106 NHP. Single screw. Taken over by Fred. Olsen, 1901. Sold to Danish owners, 1903. Wrecked, 1904.

Norway (i) (1901 – 1909)
Completed 1891 by Grangemouth Dockyard Co., Grangemouth for Dampskibsselskab Færder, Christiania. 895 gross tons. 202 ft. 8 ins b.p. x 30 ft. 1in. 3-cylinder triple-expansion steam engine by Dunsmuir & Jackson, Glasgow. 122 NHP. Single screw. Taken over by Fred. Olsen, 1901. Sold to W. Eadie, Glasgow and renamed *Cetriana*, 1909. Sold to Luke Thomas & Co., Vancouver, 1916. Sold to Cowasjee Dinshaw & Bros., Aden and Bombay, 1916. Wrecked, 1923.

Scotland (ii) (1904 -1911)
Completed 1904 by Grangemouth & Greenock Dockyard Co., Grangemouth. 1,100 gross tons. 215 ft. 5ins b.p. x 32 ft. 1in. 3-cylinder triple-expansion steam engine by Dunsmuir & Jackson, Glasgow. 138 NHP. Single screw. Wrecked, 1911.

Anvers (1906 – 1915) May have carried passengers for Fred. Olsen.
Completed 1883 by Pearce Bros., Dundee as *Commonwealth* for Commonwealth Steam Ship Co. Ltd. (Wilson & Armstrong, Newcastle). 958 gross tons. 215 ft. 0ins b.p. x 31 ft. 8ins. Iron hull. 2-cylinder compound steam engine by Pearce Bros., Dundee. 120 NHP. Single screw. Bought by Østlandske Lloyd, Christiania and renamed *Anvers*, 1895. Taken over by Fred. Olsen, 1906. Seized by German forces, 1915. Listed as owned by German Government, 1921. Bought by August Schmielau Söhne, Altona and renamed *August Schmielau*, 1922. Bought by Schiffarts "Justus" A.G., Hamburg and renamed *Marianne*, 1923. Bought by Baltische Reederei, Hamburg, 1926. Bought by Dinko Kozulic & K., Sebenico, Jugoslavia and renamed *Olib*, 1926. Bought by Kleva Simun, Istra, Jugoslavia, 1928. Scrapped, 1931.

Frigga (1906 – 1912) May have carried passengers for Fred. Olsen.
Completed 1881 by Irvine & Co., West Hartlepool as *Talley Abbey* for Pyman, Watson & Co., Cardiff. 967 gross tons. 214 ft. 5ins b.p. x 21 ft. 2ins. Iron hull. 2-cylinder compound steam engine by T. Richardson & Sons, Hartlepool. 120 NHP. Single screw. Sold to A/S Frigga, (Joh. E. v.d. Ohe, Bergen) and renamed *Frigga*, 1895. Bought by Østlandske Lloyd, Christiania, not renamed, 1898. Taken over by Fred. Olsen, 1906. Sold to A/S C. Christoffersen, Brevik, 1912. Transferred to A/S Frigga (C. Christofferson, Brevik), 1914. Later A/S Frigga (N. Malmberg, Nyköping). Torpedoed, 1917.

Memento (1906 – 1916) May have carried passengers for Fred. Olsen.
Completed 1884 by Campbell, Mackintosh & Boustead, Newcastle upon Tyne as *Danehill* for Hay, Adams & Co., Liverpool. 1,117 gross tons. 220 ft. 6ins b.p. x 35 ft. 1in. Iron hull. 2-cylinder compound steam engine by Wallsend Slipway Co. Ltd., Newcastle upon Tyne. 124 NHP. Single screw. Sold to Danehill Steamship Co., Ltd. (H. Andrews, Newcastle upon Tyne), 1886. Transferred to Warkworth Ship Co., Ltd. (H. Andrews, Newcastle upon Tyne), 1892. Bought by Østlandske Lloyd, Christiania and renamed *Memento*, 1898. Taken over by Fred. Olsen, 1906. Torpedoed, 1916.

Sovereign (1906 – 1912)
Completed 1886 by Raylton Dixon & Co., Middlesbrough as *African* for Union Steamship Co., Ltd. 1,397 gross tons. 244 ft. 2ins b.p. x 33ft. 4ins. 3-cylinder triple-expansion steam engine by T. Richardson & Sons, Hartlepool. 185 NHP. Single screw. Sold to F. H. Powell & Co., Ltd., Liverpool and renamed *Graceful*, 1893. Bought by Østlandske Lloyd and renamed *Sovereign*, 1902. Taken over by Fred. Olsen, 1906. Sold to Det Bergenske Dampskibsselskab and renamed *Zeta*, 1912. Scrapped, 1931.

Sterling (i) (1906)
Completed 1890 by S. & H. Morton & Co., Leith for Østlandske Lloyd, Christiania. 1,034 gross tons. 210 ft. 0ins b.p. x 30 ft. 1in. 3-cylinder triple-expansion steam engine by S. & H. Morton & Co., Leith. 127 NHP. Single screw. Taken over by Fred. Olsen, 1906. Sold to A/S Dampskibselskab Thore (Thor E. Tulinius, Copenhagen) but not renamed, 1906. Sold to Rederi A/B Artemis (Otto Hellsten, Stockholm) and renamed *Themis*, 1915. Sold to Government of Iceland for whom managed by H.f. Eimskipatelag Islands and renamed *Sterling*, 1917. Wrecked, 1922.

Sterling (ii) (1907 – 1922)
Completed 1907 by Fredriksstad Mekaniske Verksted, Fredriksstad. 1,323 gross tons. 231 ft. 4ins b.p. x 34 ft. 1in. 3-cylinder triple-expansion steam engine by Fredriksstad

Mekaniske Verksted. 175 NHP. Single screw. Wrecked, 1922.

Brüssel (1907 – 1927)
Completed 1907 by Fredriksstad Mekaniske Verksted, Fredriksstad. 1,489 gross tons. 241 ft. 7ins b.p. (244 ft. 8ins. o.a.) x 35 ft. 1in. 3-cylinder triple-expansion steam engine by Fredriksstad Mekaniske Verksted. 150 NHP. Single screw. Sold to Suomen Höyrylaiva OY (i.e.: the Finland Line), Helsinki and renamed *Norma*, 1927. Scrapped, 1964.

Brabant (i) (1907 – 1917)
Completed 1907 by Fredriksstad Mekaniske Verksted, Fredriksstad. 1,492 gross tons. 241 ft. 6ins b.p. x 35 ft. 1in. 3-cylinder triple-expansion steam engine by Fredriksstad Mekaniske Verksted. 150 NHP. Single screw. Sank after hitting a mine, 1917.

Paris (i) (1910-1917)
Completed 1910 by Akers Mekaniske Verksted, Christiania. 1,634 gross tons. 241 ft. 6ins b.p. x 37 ft. 3ins. 3-cylinder triple-expansion steam engine by Akers Mekaniske Verksted. 169 NHP. Single screw. Torpedoed, 1917.

Norway (ii) (1910 – 1917)
Completed 1910 by Nylands Verksted, Christiania. 1,447 gross tons. 231 ft. 10ins b.p. x 35 ft. 8ins. 3-cylinder triple-expansion steam engine by Nylands Verksted. 188 NHP. Single screw. Torpedoed, 1917.

Scotland (iii) (1912 – 1916)
Completed 1912 by Nylands Verksted, Christiania. 1,490 gross tons. 231 ft. 10ins b.p. x 35 ft. 8ins. 3-cylinder triple-expansion steam engine by Nylands Verksted. 188 NHP. Single screw. Wrecked, 1916.

Bessheim (1912 – 1941)
Completed 1912 by Nylands Verksted, Christiania. 1,781 gross tons. 256 ft. 0ins b.p. x 36 ft. 2ins. 3-cylinder triple-expansion steam engine by Nylands Verksted. 225 NHP. Single screw. Torpedoed, 1941.

Oscarsborg 1 (1919 – 1953)
Completed 1904 by W. Lindbergs A/B, Stockholm as *Styrsö 1* for Styrsö Bådhusaktiebolaget, Gothenburg. 151 gross tons (later 191). 99 ft.0ins b.p. x 22 ft. 5ins. 2-cylinder compound steam engine by W. Lindbergs A/B. 24 NHP. Single screw. Bought by Næsodden Dampskibsselskab, Christiania, 1911. Bought by Borgå Dampskibsselskab, an Olsen company, 1919, but still managed by the Næsodden company and their successors. Sold to John & Nils Nilsen, Fredrikstad, 1953. Reported to have been bought by Reidar K. Olsen, Svelvik, re-engined and converted into the cargo vessel *Reigun*, 1954. (Does not, however, appear as such in *Lloyd's Register*).

Paris (ii) (1922 – 1945)
Completed 1922 by Akers Mekaniske Verksted, Christiania. 1,753 gross tons. 255 ft. 8ins b.p. x 39 ft. 8ins. 3-cylinder triple-expansion steam engine by Akers Mekaniske Verksted. 169 NHP. Single screw. Requisitioned by the German authorities, 1940, and used as a transport and later as a minesweeper mother ship. Torpedoed by the British, 1945.

Biarritz (1922 -1940)
Completed 1922 by Akers Mekaniske Verksted, Christiania. 1,752 gross tons. 255 ft. 8ins b.p. x 39 ft. 8ins. 3-cylinder triple-expansion steam engine by Akers Mekaniske Verksted. 169 NHP. Single screw. Sank after striking a mine, 1940.

Blenheim (i) (1923 – 1941)
Completed 1923 by Nylands Verksted, Christiania. 1,807 gross tons. 256 ft. 0ins b.p. x 36 ft. 1in. 3-cylinder, triple-expansion steam engine by Nylands Verksted. 225 NHP. Single screw. Requisitioned by the German authorities, 1940, and used as a troopship. Destroyed by fire, 1941.

Brabant (iii) (1926 – 1954)
Completed 1926 by Akers Mekaniske Verksted, Oslo. 2,335 gross tons. 270 ft. 6ins b.p. (282 ft. 0ins. o.a.) x 41 ft. 2ins. Two 6-cylinder Burmeister & Wain diesel engines by Akers Mekaniske Verksted. 446 NHP. Twin screw. Requisitioned by the German authorities, 1940, and used as a transport. Returned to Olsens, 1945. Sold to Sudan Navigation Co., renamed *Suakin*, 1954. Sold to Hussein Mohamed Fayez & Sons, Jeddah and renamed *Radwa*, 1971. Scrapped, 1972.

Bali (1935 – 1952)
Completed 1928 by Swan, Hunter & Wigham Richardson, Newcastle as *Alnwick* for the Tyne-Tees Steam Shipping Co., Ltd., Newcastle. 1,428 gross tons. 254 ft. 0in b.p. x 38 ft. 10ins. 3-cylinder triple-expansion steam engine by Swan, Hunter & Wigham Richardson. 392 NHP. Single screw. Purchased by Olsens, 1935. Requisitioned by the German authorities, 1940, and used as a transport, later as a minesweeper. Returned to Olsens, 1945. Sold to the Burmese Shipping Board and renamed *Pyidawtha*, 1952. Wrecked, 1955.

Bretagne (iii) (1937 – 1958)
Completed 1937 by Akers Mekaniske Verksted, Oslo. 3,285 gross tons. 299 ft. 10ins b.p. (315 ft. 1in. o.a.) x 46 ft. 3ins. 9-cylinder Burmeister & Wain diesel engine by Akers Mekaniske Verksted. 608 NHP. Single screw. Requisitioned by the German authorities, 1941, and used as an accommodation ship, later as a transport. Returned to Olsens, 1945. Sold to Hellenic Mediterranean Lines, Piraeus and renamed *Massalia*, 1958. Scrapped, 1974.

Black Prince (i) (1938 – 1941)
Completed 1938 by Akers Mekaniske Verksted, Oslo. 5,039 gross tons. 365 ft. 2ins b.p. x 53 ft. 4ins. Two 9-cylinder Burmeister & Wain diesel engines by Akers Mekaniske Verksted. 1,215 NHP. Twin screw. Requisitioned by the German authorities, 1940, and used as an accommodation ship, later as a depot ship. Renamed *Lofoten*. Damaged by fire, 1941. Projected rebuilding, 1946-47, at first for Olsens and later for Sigurd Herlofson, abandoned. Scrapped, 1951.

Black Watch (i) (1938 – 1945)
Completed 1938 by Akers Mekaniske Verksted, Oslo. 5,035 gross tons. 365 ft. 2ins b.p. x 53 ft. 4ins. Two 9-cylinder Burmeister & Wain diesel engines by Akers Mekaniske Verksted. 1,215 NHP. Twin screw. Requisitioned by the German authorities, 1940, and used as an accommodation ship. Bombed and sunk, 1945.

Blenheim (ii) (1951 – 1968)
Completed 1951 by Akers Mekaniske Verksted, Oslo (hull and superstructure built by John I. Thornycroft & Co., Ltd., Southampton). 4,766 gross tons. 374 ft. 0ins. o.a. x 53 ft. 3ins. 8-cylinder Burmeister & Wain diesel engine by Akers

Mekansiske Verksted. 4,600 BHP. Single screw. Damaged by fire, 1968. Sold to A/S Uglands Rederi, Grimstad, 1968, and converted into car-carrier *Cilaos*. Transferred to Ocean Car Carriers Pte, Ltd., Singapore, 1974. Scrapped, 1981.

Braemar (i) (1953 – 1975)
Completed 1953 by Akers Mekaniske Verksted, Oslo (hull and superstructure built by John I. Thornycroft & Co., Ltd., Southampton). 4,776 gross tons. 374 ft. 0ins. o.a. x 53 ft. 3ins. 8-cylinder Burmeister & Wain diesel engine by Akers Mekaniske Verksted. 4,600 BHP. Single screw. Sold to Dashwood Finance Co., Ltd., London and converted into a casino ship, *The Philippine Tourist*, 1975. Transferred to Peninsula Tourist Shipping Co., Manila, 1978 and renamed *Philippine Tourist I*, 1978. Scrapped, 1980.

Black Watch (ii) (1966 - 1986)
Completed 1966 by Lübecker Flender Werke, Lübeck for the joint ownership of Fred. Olsen, for whom she sailed as *Black Watch (ii)*, and Det Bergenske Dampskibsselskab, for whom she sailed as *Jupiter*. 9,500 gross tons. 464 ft. 8ins. o.a. x 66 ft. 6ins. Two V18-cylinder Pielstick diesel engines by Ottensener Eisenwerk, Hamburg. 16,740 BHP. Twin screw. Complete ownership assumed by Det Bergenske Dampskibsselskab, 1986. Sold to Norway Line A/S, Bergen for whom she sailed as Jupiter, 1986. Sold to a subsidiary of Marlines SA, Piraeus and re-named *Crown M.*, 1990. Renamed Byblos, 2000. Renamed *Crown*, 2005. Now stationed at Dubai as an accommodation vessel.

Black Prince (ii) (1966 -)
Completed 1966 by Lübecker Flender Werke, Lübeck. 9,500 gross tons. 464 ft. 8ins. o.a. x 66 ft. 6ins. Two V18-cylinder Pielstick diesel engines by Ottensener Eisenwerk, Hamburg. 16,470 BHP. Twin screw. Det Bergenske Dampskibsselskab bought a share in her, 1968, and when sailing for them she now bore the name *Venus* but remained *Black Prince* when sailing for Olsens. Complete ownership resumed by Olsens, 1986. Reconstruction as a cruise ship completed by Wärtsilä, Turkü, 1987. Now 11,209 gross tons.

Skagen / Borgholm (iv) (1968 – 1981)
Completed 1958 by A/S Pusnes Mekaniske Verksted, Arendal for A/S Kristiansands Dampskipsselskap (KDS). 1,831 gross tons. 264 ft. 11ins o.a. x 45 ft. 5ins. Two 12-cylinder diesel engines by Nordberg Manufacturing Co., Milwaukee. 5,480 BHP. Twin screw. KDS bought by Olsens, 1968. Transferred to Fred. Olsen & Co. and renamed *Borgholm (iv)* for conversion into a depôt ship for submersibles for Fred. Olsen Oceanics, 1975. Sold to Partrederi Norghol, Drammen and renamed *Norghol*, 1981. Over the next few years, she variously passed through the hands of Norwegian Petroleum Exploration Consultants A/S, Oslo; Cob Line International A/S, Drammen; and Partrederi Norghol, Drammen. Sold to Globetrotter SA, Drammen and renamed *Pan Trader* (sometimes *Pantrader*), 1988

Christian IV (1968 – 1984)
Completed 1968 by Aalborg Vaerft A/S, Aalborg for A/S Kristiansands Dampskibsselskap (KDS). 2,681 gross tons. 308 ft. 2ins o.a. x 53 ft. 2ins. Four 12-cylinder diesel engines by A/S Holeby Dieselmotor, Holeby. 6,500 BHP. Twin screw. KDS bought by Olsens, 1968. Sold to Perbadanan Nasional Shipping Line Berhad, Kuala Lumpur and renamed *Pernas Safari*, 1985. Sold to Safari Lines, Ltd., Malta and renamed *Safari*, 1994. Sold to Porto Santo Line – Trasportes

Maritimos, Ltda., Funchal and renamed *Lobo Marinho*, 1996. Became *Lobo Marinho 1* (registered Alexcafi Commercio de Importacao e Exportacao Ltda, Funchal), 2003. Transfered to Cabo Verde Lines (Sociedad Trasportes Maritimos Cabo Verdiana, São Vicente) and renamed *Lobo dos Mares*, 2004. Sold to North Korean owners and renamed *Menhir*, 2005.

København (1968 - 1973)
Completed 1966 by Orenstein-Koppel & Lübecker Maschinenbau, Lübeck for Den Norske Københavnlinje (Sverre Ditlev-Simonsen & Co., Oslo). 3,612 gross tons. 308 ft. 2ins o.a. x 53 ft. 2ins. Two 8-cylinder Pielstick diesel engines by A/B Lindholmens Varv, Gothenburg. 6,500 BHP. Twin screw. Olsens acquired a part share, 1968. Sold to Empresa Nacional del Estado, Valparaiso and renamed *Presidente Aguirre Cerda*, 1973. Renamed *Puerto Montt*, 1974. Transferred to the Chilean Navy and renamed *Angamos*, 1976. Sold to Greek owners, 1993, but damaged by fire and scrapped.

Blenheim (iii) (1970 – 1981)
Completed 1970 by Upper Clyde Shipbuilders, Ltd., Clydebank. 10,420 gross tons. 490 ft. 1in. o.a. x 65 ft. 8ins. Two V18-cylinder Pielstick diesel engines by Crossley Premier Engines, Ltd., Manchester. 18,000 BHP. Twin screw. Sold to Scandinavian World Cruises, Miami (Det Forenede Dampskib Selskab, Copenhagen), 1981, and renamed *Scandinavian Sea*, 1982. Sold to Antonios Lelakis, Piraeus after being seriously damaged by fire, 1984. Sold to Pan Ocean Navigation Inc., Panama and renamed *Venus Venturer*, 1984. Renamed *Discovery 1*, 1986, subsequently being sold to Bajamar Shipping, Ltd., Panama and later Discovery Cruise Line Partnership, Panama. Damaged by fire and scrapped, 1996.

Buenavista (ii) / Bismillah (iii) (1971 – 2006)
Completed 1971 by Ulstein Mekaniske Verksted, Ulsteinvik for KDS. 2,714 gross tons. 311 ft. 6ins o.a. x 53 ft. 5ins. Two 8-cylinder diesel engines by Stork Werkspoor, Amsterdam. 8,800 BHP. Twin screw. Lengthened, 1974. 3,282 gross tons and 349 ft. 2ins o.a. Sold to Amsterdamse Maritiem Transport Maats. BV, Amsterdam, 1977. Bought by Comarit and renamed *Bismillah (iii)*, 1984. Gross tonnage later re-assessed as 5,213. Sold to Mexican owners and renamed *El Arcangel*, 2006.

Bonanza (ii) / Benchijigua (ii) / Bajamar (iii) (1972 - 2001)
Completed 1972 by Ulstein Mekaniske Verksted, Ulsteinvik for KDS. 2,699 gross tons. 310 ft. 8ins o.a. x 53 ft. 4ins. Two 8-cylinder diesel engines by Stork Werkspoor, Amsterdam. 8,800 BHP. Twin screw. Transferred to Ferry Gomera SA and renamed *Benchijigua (ii)*, 1980. Gross tonnage later re-assessed as 4,311. Renamed *Bajamar (iii)*, 1994. Renamed *Blessed Mother* but sale to Philippine owners fell through, 2001. No owners listed in *Lloyd's Register* until 2003 when appears as *The Blessed Mother* of MBRS Lines, Inc., Manila. Bought by Açorline, Ponta Delgada, The Azores and renamed *Cachalote*, 2003.

Bolero (1973 – 1990)
Completed 1973 by Dubigeon – Normandie S.A., Nantes. 11,344 gross tons. 466 ft. 4ins o.a. x 72 ft. 1in. Two V12-cylinder Pielstick diesel engines by Chantiers de l'Atlantique, St. Nazaire. 20,400 BHP. Twin screw. Renamed *Scandinavica*, 1978. Renamed *Bolero*, 1982. Sold to Color

Line A/S, Oslo and renamed *Jupiter*, 1990. Renamed *Crucero Express*, 1994. Renamed *Seminole Express*, 1998. Sold to Caspi Shipping, Haifa and renamed *Magic 1*, 1999. Renamed *Mirage 1*, 2003.

Benchijigua (i) / Betancuria (ii) (1974 - 1982)
Completed 1974 by Trondheims Mekaniske Verksted A/S, Trondheim for Ferry Gomera. 887 gross tons. 223 ft. 2ins o.a. x 37 ft, 9ins. Two 6-cylinder diesel engines by Nydqvist & Holm, Trollhättan. 2,310 BHP. Twin screw. Re-named *Betancuria (ii)*, 1980. Sold and renamed *Comera*, 1982, becoming *Akraborg* of H/f Skallagrimur, Akranes, Iceland. Sold to Slysavarnarfelag Islands, Reykjavik and renamed *Saebjorg*, 1998.

Borgen (ii) (1975 – 1990)
Completed 1975 by Aalborg Vaerft A/S, Aalborg. 5,330 gross tons. 357 ft 7ins o.a. x 62 ft. 4ins. Four 6-cylinder diesel engines by Stork-Werkspoor, Amsterdam. 16,000 BHP. Twin screw. Reconstructed, 1982, Now 7,570 gross tons and 427 ft. 2ins o.a. x 64 ft. 10ins. Sold to Color Line A/S, Oslo and renamed *Skagen*, 1990. Sold to Boudi Marine Co., SA, Panama and renamed *Fedra*, 2005. Bought by Arab Bridge Maritime Co., Aqaba, 2005.

Bolette (vi) / Boughaz (1984 -)
Completed 1974 by Jos. L. Meyer, Papenburg as *Viking 5* for Rederi A/B Sally, Mariehamn. 5,288 gross tons. 386 ft. 5 ins o.a. x 56 ft. 7ins. Originally two V14-cylinder diesel engines by NV Mach. Bolnes. Twin screw. Renamed *The Viking*, 1981 and *Sally Express*, 1983. Re-engined with two V12-cylinder diesel engines by Klöckner Humboldt Deutz, Cologne. 800 KW. Bought by Olsens and renamed *Bolette (vi)*, 1984. Transferred to Comarit and renamed *Boughaz*, 1988. Gross tonnage re-assessed as 8,257.

Braemar (ii) (1985 – 1990)
Completed 1980 by OY Wärtsilä, Turkü as *Viking Song* for Rederi A/B Sally, Mariehamn. 14,623 gross tons. 476 ft. 4ins o.a. x 83 ft. 8ins. Four V12-cylinder Pielstick diesel engines by Wärtsilä. 26,000 BHP. Bought by Olsens and renamed *Braemar*, 1985. Briefly renamed *Baltika* during an aborted sale to Baltic Shipping Co., St. Petersburg, 1990, but eventually transferred to Rigorous Shipping Co., Ltd., Limassol and renamed *Anna Karenina*, 1991. Transferred to Baltic Shipping Co., St. Petersburg, 1995. Became *Anna K*, 1996. Sold to E-Line AS, Tallinn and renamed *Regina Baltica*, 1996. Subsequent owners: Estonian Shipping Co., Tallinn and then Hansatee Shipmanagement, Ltd, Tallinn.

Bonanza (iii) (1988 – 1989)
Ordered by Stena Line A/B, Gothenburg from Stoczmia im "Komuny Paryskieg", Gdynia, 1979 but still unfinished in 1988 when bought by Olsens, who proposed to name her *Bonanza (iii)*. Intended tonnage: circa 38,000 gross. Sold while still incomplete to ANEK Anonymos Naftiliaki Eteria Kritis AE, Chania and named *Kydon II*, 1989. Completed and renamed *El. Venizelos*, sometimes *Eleftherios Venizelos*, 1992.

Bayard (viii) (1989 – 1990)
Completed 1982 by A.G. Weser Seebeckwerft, Bremerhaven as *Olau Britannia* for Partenrederei m.s. "Olau Britannia" (Olau-Line (U.K.) Ltd. & Co., Hamburg). 14,983 gross tons. 503 ft. 4ins o.a. x 79 ft. 6ins. Four Pielstick 8-cylinder diesel engines by Blohm & Voss AG, Hamburg. 20,800 BHP.

Twin screw. Sold to Nordström & Thulin, 1988. Bought by Olsens and renamed *Bayard (viii)*, 1989. Sold to Color Line A/S, Oslo and renamed *Christian IV*, 1990.

Betancuria (iii) (1989 – 1995)
Completed 1966 by Storviks Mekaniske Verksted A/S, Kristiansund as *Tungenes* for Det Stavangerske Dampskibsselskab, Stavanger. 681 gross tons. 186 ft. 7ins. o.a. x 34 ft. 6ins. Two Normo 8-cylinder diesel engines by A/S Bergens Mekaniske Verksted, Bergen. 2,080 BHP. Sold to H/f Skallgrimur, Akranes, Iceland and renamed *Akraborg*, 1974. Bought by Baltic Shipping & Trading SA, Panama and renamed *Sunflower*, 1984. Bought by Ferry Gomera and renamed *Betancuria (iii)*, 1989. Sold to Jewel Line Marine, Inc., Panama and renamed *Ciudad de Melilla*, 1995. Sold to Naviera Boluda Fos SL., Las Palmas de Gran Canaria and renamed *Elisa B*, 1996. Damaged by fire, 1998, and sold for scrapping but sank while under tow.

Buganvilla (1992 – 2004)
Completed 1968 by Jos. L. Meyer, Papenburg as *Betula* for Linjebuss International A/B, Helsingborg. 2,452 gross tons. 233 ft. 11ins o.a. x 54 ft. 5ins. Four Deutz 8-cylinder diesel engines by Klöckner Humboldt Deutz, Cologne. 4,399 BHP. Twin screw. Transferred to Stockholms Rederi A/B "Svea", Stockholm, 1971. Sold to Scandinavian Ferry Lines A/B, Helsingborg, 1981. Refitted and re-engined with second hand units of a similar type, 1982. 3,686 gross tons. Bought by Ferry Gomera and renamed *Buganvilla*, 1992. Sold to Cabo Verde Lines (Sociedad Transportes Maritimos, Ltda, São Vicente, Cape Verde Islands), and renamed *Tarrafal*, 2004.

Benchijigua (iii) / Betancuria (iv) (1994 – 2002)
Completed 1974 by Schichau-Unterweser AG, Bremerhaven as *Djursland II* for Det Dansk-Franske Dampskibsselskab, (Jydsk Færgefart, Grenaa). 4,371 gross tons. 387 ft. 2ins o.a. x 60 ft. 10ins. Two MAN V12-cylinder diesel engines by Maschinenbau-Augsburg-Nuremburg, Augsburg. 13,390 BHP. Twin screw. Renamed *Djursland*, 1980. Jydsk Færgefart bought by DFDS, Copenhagen, 1981. Bought by Grenaa-Hundested Linien A/S, Grenaa, 1983. Tonnage later re-assessed at 8,531. Bought by Fred. Olsen S.A. and renamed *Benchijigua II*, 1994, and *Benchijigua (iii)*, 1995. Renamed *Betancuria (iv)*, 2000. Sold to El Salam Shipping & Trading Establishment, Cairo and renamed *Sara 1*, 2002. Chartered to Comarit, 2003.

Bañaderos (iii) / Barlovento (1994 – 2005)
Completed 1976 by Aalborg Vaerft, Aalborg as *Viking Voyager* for Stanhope Steamship, Ltd. (Townsend Car Ferries, Ltd., Dover). 6,837 gross tons. 422 ft. 7ins o.a. x 66 ft. 4ins. One 9-cylinder and two 8-cylinder diesel engines by Stork-Werkspoor Diesel BV, Amsterdam. 13,749 BHP. Triple screw. Townsend Thoresen acquired by P&O European Ferries, 1987, following which *Viking Voyager* renamed *Pride of Cherbourg*, 1989 and *Pride of Cherbourg II*, 1994. Gross tonnage re-assessed as 9,735. Bought by Fred. Olsen SA and renamed *Bañaderos*, 1994. Renamed *Barlovento*, 2000. Sold to SAOS Anonymos Naftiliaki Eteria Samothrakis, *Samothraki* and renamed Samothraki 2005.

Bahia Express (1994 – 1997)
Completed 1989 by Brødrene Aa Batbyggeri A/S, Hyen as *Sant' Agata* for Fekete & Co. A/S, Tonsberg. 395 gross tons. 116 ft. 3ins o.a. x 37 ft. 9ins. Reinforced plastic. Air cushion

ferry. Two V16-cylinder diesel engines by Motorenwerke Mannheim AG, Mannheim. 4,348 BHP. Water jets. Renamed *Wight King*, 1991. Bought by Fred. Olsen SA and renamed *Bahia Express*, 1994. Sold to Trans Universal Seas Co., Kuwait and renamed *Shahrazad Express*, 1997.

Banassa / Banasa (1996 –)
Completed 1975 by Helsingør Vaerft A/S, Helsingør as *Mette Mols* for Mols Linien A/S, Ebeltoft. 4,948 gross tons. 378 ft. 5ins o.a. x 67 ft. 7ins. Four Burmeister & Wain 6-cylinder diesel engines by Helsingør Vaerft. 16,400 BHP. Twin screw. Gross tonnage re-assessed as 11,668. Renamed *Mette Mo*, 1996. Bought by Comarit and renamed *Banassa*, 1996. *Banasa*, 1997. Re-engined with four MAN B&W 8-cylinder diesel engines, 2003. 14,792BHP.

Black Watch (iii) (1996 –)
Completed 1972 by OY Wärtsilä, Helsinki as *Royal Viking Star* for Det Bergenske Dampskibsselskab, Bergen. 21,847 gross tons. 583 ft. 1in o.a. x 82 ft. 8ins. Four Sulzer 9-cylinder diesel engines by Wärtsilä. 18,000 BHP. Twin screw. Lengthened, 1981. 28,221 gross tons. Length now 674 ft. 1in o.a. Transferred to Norwegian Cruise Line and renamed *Westward*, 1990. Transferred to Royal Cruise Line and renamed *Star Odyssey*, 1994. Bought by Olsens and renamed *Black Watch*, 1996. Re-engined with four MAN/B&W 7-cylinder diesel engines and given a major refit, 2005.

Bonanza Express (1999 –)
Completed 1999 by Incat Australia Pty., Ltd., Hobart. 5,199 gross tons. Twin hull. 315 ft. 0ins o.a. x 85 ft. 3 ins. Four Ruston V20-cylinder diesel engines by Ruston Paxman Diesels, Ltd., Colchester. 38,501 BHP. Water jets.

Bentayga Express / Bencomo Express (1999 –)
Completed 1999 by Incat Australia Pty., Ltd. Hobart initially as *Benchijigua Express* but quickly renamed *Bentayga Express*. 6,344 gross tons. Twin hull. 315 ft. 0ins o.a. x 92 ft. 5ins. Four V18-cylinder diesel engines by Caterpillar, Inc., Peroria, Illinois. 38,501 BHP. Water jets. Renamed *Bencomo Express*, 2004.

Benchijigua Express (i) / Bentago Express (2000 –)
Completed 2000 by Incat Australia Pty., Ltd. Hobart. 6,348 gross tons. Twin hull. 315 ft. 0ins o.a. x 92 ft. 5ins. Four V18-cylinder diesel engines by Caterpillar, Inc., Peeroria, Illinois. 38,501 BHP. Water jets. Renamed *Bentago Express*, 2004.

Braemar (iii) (2001 –)
Completed 1993 by Union Naval de Levante SA, Valencia as *Crown Dynasty* for Crown Cruises, then Commodore Cruise Line, Inc., Coral Gables, Florida. 19,089 gross tons. 537 ft. 6ins o.a. x 73 ft. 10 ins. Four Wärtsilä 8-cylinder diesel engines by Echevarria Wärtsilä Diesel SA, Bermeo. 17,826 BHP. Twin screw. Unofficially renamed *Cunard Dynasty* while under Cunard management. Renamed *Crown Majesty* while under charter to Majesty Cruise Line, 1997, and *Norwegian Dynasty* for a charter to Norwegian Cruise Line, also 1997. Reverted to *Crown Dynasty*, 1999. Bought by Olsens and renamed *Braemar*, 2001. To be lengthened, 2008.

Berkane (2002 –)
Completed 1976 by Dubigeon-Normandie, SA, Nantes as *Napoléon* for Société Nationale Maritime Corse Méditerranée, Marseilles. 20,079 gross tons. 508 ft. 7ins o.a. x 78 ft. 10 ins. Two Pielstick V18-cylinder diesel engines by Chantiers de l'Atlantique, St. Nazaire. 35,218 BHP. Twin screw. Bought by Comarit and renamed *Berkane*, 2002.

Bocayna Express (2003 –)
Completed 2003 by Austal Ships Pty., Ltd., Fremantle. 2,578 gross tons. Twin hull. 217 ft. 2ins o.a. x 61 ft. 2ins. Two V18-cylinder and two V12-cylinder diesel engines by Paxman Diesels, Ltd., Colchester. 15,772 BHP. Water jets.

Biladi (2003 –)
Completed 1980 by Dubigeon-Normandie SA, Nantes as *Liberté* for Société Nationale Maritime Corse Méditerranée. 10,766 gross tons. 464 ft. 2ins o.a. x 71ft. 2ins. Two Pielstick V18-cylinder diesel engines by Chantiers de l'Atlantique, St. Nazaire. 23,414 BHP. Lengthened, 1991. Now 18,913 gross tons and 539 ft. 4ins o.a. Bought by Comarit and renamed *Biladi*, 2003.

Benchijigua Express (ii) (2005 –)
Completed 2005 by Austal Ships Pty., Ltd., Fremantle. 8,089 gross tons. 415 ft. 8ins o.a. x 99 ft. 9ins. Triple hull. Four 20-cylinder diesel engines by MTU Friedrichshafen GmbH, Friedrichshafen. 44,596 BHP. Water jets.

Boudicca (2005 –)
Completed 1973 by OY Wärtsilä, Helsinki as *Royal Viking Sky* for Det Nordenfjeldske Dampskibsselskab, Trondheim. 21,891 gross tons. 583 ft. 3ins o.a. x 82 ft. 7ins. Four Sulzer 9-cylinder diesel engines by Wärtsilä. 18,000 BHP. Twin screw. Lengthened, 1982. Now 28,078 gross tons and 674 ft. 1in. Transferred to Norwegian Cruise Line and renamed *Sunward*, 1991. Sold to Birka Cruise, Ltd., Stockholm and renamed *Birka Queen*, 1992, and *Golden Princess* (for charter to Princess Cruises), 1993. Bought by Star Cruise Sendirian Berhad, Pulau Pinang and renamed *Superstar Capricorn*, 1996. Renamed *Hyundai Kumgang* (for charter to Hyundai Merchant Marine Co.), 1998. *Superstar Capricorn*, 2001. Bought by Grand Latino de Navegaçion SA (Iberojet, Barcelona) and renamed *Grand Latino*, 2004. Bought by Olsens, re-engined (four MAN/B&W 7-cylinder diesels) and renamed *Boudicca*, 2005.

Balmoral (2006 –)
Completed 1988 by Jos. L. Meyer, Papenburg as *Crown Odyssey* for Royal Cruise Line, San Francisco and Piraeus. 34,242 gross tons. 615 ft. 10ins o.a. x 92 ft. 6ins. Two MaK 8-cylinder and two MaK 6-cylinder diesel engines by Krupp MaK Maschinenbau GmbH, Kiel. 28,955 BHP. Twin screw, Transferred to Norwegian Cruise Line and renamed *Norwegian Crown*, 1996. Transferred to Orient Lines and renamed *Crown Odyssey*, 2000. Transferred back to Norwegian Cruise Line and renamed *Norwegian Crown*, 2003. Bought by Olsens, 2006. Lengthened and renamed *Boudicca*, 2007. Now 715 ft. 7ins o.a.

Index

More fine books from Carmania Press.

PASSENGER LINERS SCANDINAVIAN STYLE by Bruce Peter.
Hardback. 176 pages. 25 colour and 189 black & white illustrations. **£27-00**
LINERS & CRUISE SHIPS: Some Notable Smaller Vessels by Anthony Cooke.
Softback. 136 pages. 169 black & white illustrations. **£12-95**
LINERS & CRUISE SHIPS – 2: Some More Notable Smaller Vessels by Anthony Cooke.
Softback. 113 pages. 137 black & white illustrations. **£13-95**
LINERS & CRUISE SHIPS – 3: Further Notable Smaller Vessels by Anthony Cooke.
Softback. 160 pages. 32 colour and 124 black & white illustrations. **£18-95**
LINERS OF THE GOLDEN AGE by William H. Miller, Anthony Cooke and Maurizio Eliseo.
Large format hardback. 240 pages. 229 black & white illustrations. **£35-00**
OCEAN LINER CHRONICLES by William H. Miller.
Softback. 136 pages. 13 colour and 162 black & white illuistrations. **£16-95**
PASSENGER LINERS AMERICAN STYLE by William H. Miller.
Softback. 160 pages. 230 black & white illustrations. **£15-95**
PASSENGER LINERS FRENCH STYLE by William H. Miller.
Softback. 140 pages. 253 black & white illustrations. **£16-95**
THE LAST WHITE EMPRESSES: Canadian Pacific's post-War Atlantic liners. by Clive Harvey.
Softback. 120 pages. 37 colour and 72 black & white illustrations. **£17-95**
THE SAXONIA SISTERS: Cunard's Canadian liners. by Clive Harvey.
Softback. 96 pages. 18 colour and 79 black & white illustrations. **£13-95**
CUNARDER Maritime paintings by Stephen J. Card.
Landscape format hardback. 176 pages. 40 colour paintings. 9 pen & ink drawings. 16 colour photographs. **£36-00**
HOLLAND AMERICA LINE: THE SPOTLESS FLEET Maritime paintings by Stephen J. Card.
Landscape format hardback. 224 pages. 84 colour paintings. 16 pen & ink drawings. **£36-00**
THE SITMAR LINERS AND THE V. SHIPS, 1928-1998 by Maurizio Eliseo.
Hardback. 262 pages. 60 colour and 250 black & white illustrations. Plans and profiles. **£17-50**
SEVEN SEAS NAVIGATOR: Six Stars on the Ocean Souvenir book by Maurizio Eliseo.
Hardback. 108 pages. 226 colour and 26 black & white illustrations. **£32-50**
LINERS TO THE SUN by John Maxtone-Graham. (2nd edition)
Softback. 495 pages. 252 black & white illustrations. (not for sale in U.S.A. or Canada) **£10-00**
OCEAN LINER ODYSSEY, 1958-1969 by Theodore W. Scull.
Softback. 88 pages. 132 black & white illustrations. **£10-95**
SOUTHAMPTON SHIPPING (with Portsmouth, Poole & Weymouth) A photographic survey. by R. Bruce Grice and David F. Hutchings.
Large format hardback. 212 pages. 25 colour and 148 black & white illustrations. **£32-00**
Laurence Dunn's THAMES SHIPPING. A photographic survey. (4th impression)
Softback. 112 pages. 280 black & white illustrations. **£13-95**
Laurence Dunn's MEDITERRANEAN SHIPPING. A photographic survey.
Softback. 132 pages. 322 black & white illustrations. **£15-95**
MERCHANT SHIPS OF A BYGONE ERA: THE POST-WAR YEARS by William H. Miller.
(2nd impression) *Softback. 136 pages. 203 black & white illustrations.* **£14-95**
THE NURSE FAMILY OF BRIDGWATER AND THEIR SHIPS by James Nurse.
Softback. 36 pages. 27 black & white illustrations. **£5-95**

CARMANIA PRESS. PO Box 56435, London, SE3 0SZ.
'Phone: 0208-852-1236.
e-mail: anthonycooke@carmania.F9.co.uk web-site: www.carmaniapress.co.uk